The
Year
of the
Poet XII

August 2025

The Poetry Posse

inner child press, ltd.

'building bridges of cultural understanding'

i

The Poetry Posse 2025

Gail Weston Shazor

Shareef Abdur Rasheed

Teresa E. Gallion

hülya n. yılmaz

Noreen Snyder

Tzemin Ition Tsai

Elizabeth Esguerra Castillo

Jackie Davis Allen

Mutawaf Shaheed

Caroline 'Ceri' Nazareno

Ashok K. Bhargava

Alicja Maria Kuberska

Swapna Behera

Albert 'Infinite' Carrasco

Kimberly Burnham

Eliza Segiet

William S. Peters, Sr.

~ * ~

In order to maintain each poet's authentic voice, this volume has not undergone the scrutiny of editing. Please take time to indulge each contributor for their own creativity and aspirations to convey their uniqueness.

hülya n. yılmaz, Ph.D.
Director of Editing ~
Inner Child Press International

The Year of the Poet XII
August 2025 Edition

The Poetry Posse

1st Edition : 2025

This Publishing is protected under Copyright Law as a "Collection". All rights for all submissions are retained by the Individual Author and or Artist. No part of this Publishing may be Reproduced, Transferred in any manner without the prior **WRITTEN CONSENT** of the "Material Owners" or its Representative Inner Child Press. Any such violation infringes upon the Creative and Intellectual Property of the Owner pursuant to International and Federal Copyright Laws. Any queries pertaining to this "Collection" should be addressed to Publisher of Record.

Publisher Information

1st Edition : Inner Child Press
intouch@innerchildpress.com
www.innerchildpress.com

Copyright © 2025 : The Poetry Posse

ISBN-13 : 978-1-961498-70-9 (inner child press, ltd.)

$ 12.99

WHAT WOULD LIFE BE WITHOUT A LITTLE POETRY?

Dedication

This Book is dedicated to

Humanity, Peace & Poetry

the Power of the Pen

can effectuate change!

&

The Poetry Posse

past, present & future,

our Patrons and Readers &

the Spirit of our Everlasting Muse

In the darkness of my life
I heard the music
I danced . . .
and the Light appeared
and I dance

Janet P. Caldwell

Table of Contents

Connection ~ Fulfillment ~ Hope

The Poetry Posse

Table of Contents . . . *continued*

Foreword

Connection ~ Fulfillment ~ Hope

Embracing the Heartbeat of Life: A Journey
Through Poetry

I am elated to write the Foreword for the August
2025 Edition of the Year of the Poet.

There's something magical about poetry—it has this
unique way of reaching into our souls and pulling
out emotions we sometimes struggle to name. This
collection is all about those *deep connections* we
share, the sense of *fulfillment* that keeps us moving
forward, and the ever-present spark of *hope* that
lights even the darkest paths.

Whether you're seeking comfort, inspiration, or
simply a moment to reflect, these poems invite you
to:

- Celebrate the bonds that tie us together
- Explore what it means to find true
  fulfillment
- Hold onto hope, no matter the challenges
  ahead

In yet another beautiful and enchanting collection of
verses, The Poetry Posse and our Featured Poets for
the Month of August takes you to the various depths

of human emotions as depicted in their evocative and inspiring compositions.

My congratulations once again to my Poetry Posse Family spearheaded by William S. Peters, Sr., to the Poetry Posse, and to our Featured Poets of the Month!

So, take a deep breath, open your heart, and let's dive into words that remind us we're never truly alone on this journey.

Elizabeth Esguerra Castillo
International Author/Poet/Visual Artist

Preface

We, **Inner Child Press International, The Year of the Poet** and **The Poetry Posse** welcome you.

As we now are in our 12th year of monthly publications for **The Year of the Poet**, we continue to be excited.

This particular year we have chosen to feature a collection of human emotions. We do hope you enjoy the poet's perspectives on these subjects. Read ~ Learn.

For those of you who are not familiar with our story, back in 2013, a few of us poets got together with the simple intention of producing a book a month. That was our challenge. Since that time the enterprise has blossomed and brought forth a fruit that seems to keep on growing as evidenced as we enter 2023.

Our purpose is simple. Through our lyrical words and verse, we not only wish to share our poetic works, but we also have the poetic naiveté to believe that we can assist in the growth of consciousness of the things that have an effect our collective humanity. Therefore, we welcome your readership. For more about what we are attempting to accomplish, have a look at our Publishing Web Site . . . www.innerchildpress.com. If you would like to

know a bit more about this particular endeavor please stop by for a visit at :
www.innerchildpress.com/the-year-of-the-poet

Over the years, Inner Child Press has been socially active to bring awareness and catalog through literature the things that have an impact upon our world and its inhabitants. We have solicited, produced, underwritten and published quite a few volumes to that end. For more insight you may wish to visit : www.innerchildpress.com/the-anthology-market. If you are a writer, poet, or activist, you would be advised to keep a eye out for upcoming volumes should you desire to participate. All readers are welcomed as well. Note, that there is a myriad of published volumes that are available as a FREE PDF download as well as available for purchase at affordable prices.

We at this time extend to you our well wishes for your own personal journey and hope that you consider including us as a travel companion.

Bless Up

Bill

William S. Peters, Sr.

Publisher
Inner Child Press International
www.innerchildpress.com

Connection	Fulfillment	Hope
Sunflowers	Lotus	Daffodils

In July, the Inner Child Poetry Posse shared our thoughts on Nostalgia, Wisdom and Fearlessness. This month in *The Year Of The Poet* we look at the similar but more forward thinking theme of "Hope" for the future. We are rising into the future as opposed to remembering past experiences.

As Maya Angelou says in *Still I Rise*, "Just like moons and like suns, / With the certainty of tides, / Just like hopes springing high, / Still I'll rise."

I love this line, "with the certainty of tides." It evokes certainty and hope in the natural world as well as an expectation of permanence or predictability of something that is fluid and fluctuating. Our poems represent the idea of balancing life and death, certainty and chaos, and hope and disappointment.

Another theme is "Fulfilment", which often goes hand in hand with wisdom. Fulfilment comes from making wise choices and dreaming of how to create a better world. As poets, we dream big and here we share what brings us a sense of fulfillment and hope. We imagine the future we would create if we were all powerful.

We imagine as in the poems of fulfillment from Lao Tzu, "Empty your mind of all thoughts. Let your heart be at peace. … When you realize where you come from, you naturally become tolerant, disinterested, amused, kindhearted as a grandmother, dignified as a king."

We come from so many places, people and experiences.

Bringing it all together is the third theme "Connection." Where do you come from? Where do you connect to others? Is it a place, a where or is it a way, a how? How do you connect to others?

We hope that these poems stimulate you to wonder at hope in the future, the fulfillment of dreams and the ways we are all connected.

Kimberly Burnham

Integrative Medicine
Spokane Washington

Poets . . .
sowing seeds in the
Conscious Garden of Life,
that those who have yet to come
may enjoy the Flowers.

Poets, Writers . . . know that we are the enchanting magicians that nourishes the seeds of dreams and thoughts . . . it is our words that entice the hearts and minds of others to believe there is something grand about the possibilities that life has to offer and our words tease it forth into action . . . for you are the Poet, the Writer to whom the Gift of Words has been entrusted . . .

~ wsp

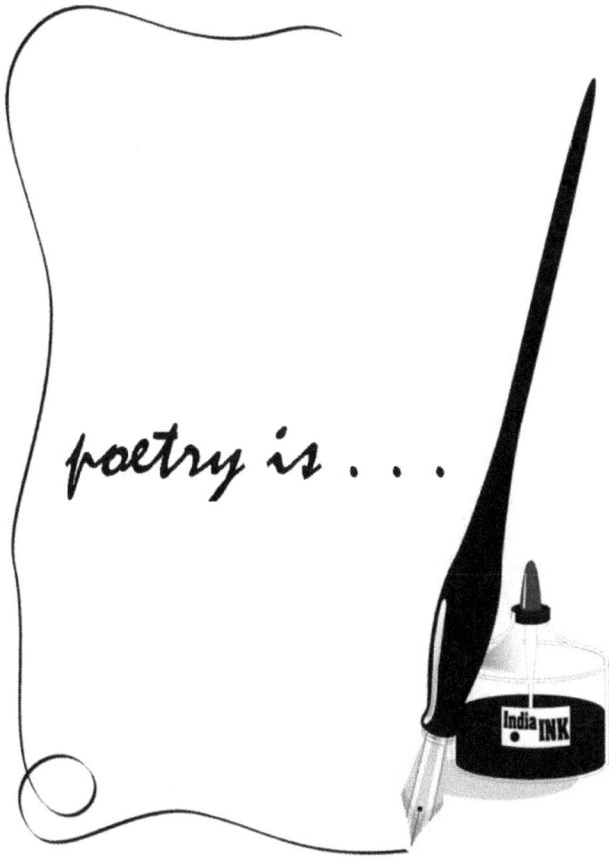

poetry is . . . .

Poetry succeeds where instruction fails.

~ wsp

Coming Soon

www.innerchildpress.com

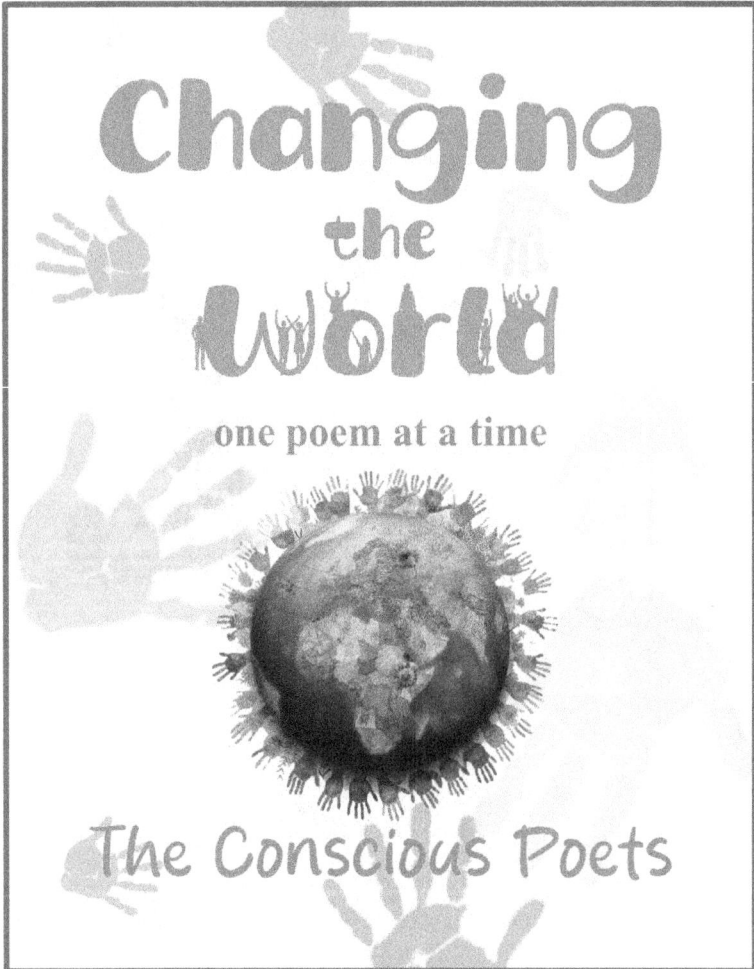

Changing the World

one poem at a time

The Conscious Poets

Gail Weston Shazor

Gail Weston Shazor

Gail Weston Shazor is a lover of words. She is fond of the arcane, unusual and the not yet words.

Coining words at an early age, there was often a bit of trouble with teachers, but she always had her mother and aunt to back up her choices in expression. Born in Mississippi, she spent her early years with her grandparents. Each of the four left very careful influences on her pre-schooling. She learned in turn how women worked in and out of the home and how men worked in and out of the home to support the family. She learned that a lack of proper schooling was not the only way to learn and understanding life was a great teacher. As in most rural families of color, women had a greater chance of formal learning. Both of Gail's grandmothers read out loud to the family whether it was the bible or the newspapers and important documents to their spouses.

Gail Weston Shazor has authored (so far) Notes from the Blue Roof, A Overstanding of an Imperfect Love, HeartSongs and Lies My Grandfather's Told Me. The number of anthologies is too many to list with the premier accomplishment of one of the contributors to The Year of The Poet. Gail will always lend her ink to community projects and will purchase the books of fellow poets in the Inner Child Press family.

Blue Roof #23

Lie with me on this rooftop
Smooth my scalp
From the nape of neck
To my brow
I am powerless to stop
Remembrances
Of the pure blue pleasure that comes
From being
Touched
By caring hands
Ministered to in moments
Of weakness, clarity
Vulnerability
At the moment in between
Yes and no
Alone and attended
It is in this blue space
That I come to realize
I may never be touched
Again
Simply
Without reservation, wholly
As one who is wanted
Or even as one who is convenient
For the moment
Run your fingers across my
Exposed back
Unguarded to your touch
And in a lazy fashion
I will sigh
Drawing that much closer to you
Whisper to me
I will not care of what

Just that it matters to you
These stories
In the telling
I will become wiser
For the knowing
And it will be as poignant
A lie
As the ones I had previously known
When my life was changed
Without the notice
Of your pending withdrawal
The sober navy changes
To a washed out place
Matching the knowledge of
No longer being

Blue Roof #22

You spread your fingers
Across the spaces
Between my ribs
My agitation calms
Beneath your gift
The need precedes
The grace of your presence
And I am reminded
That you are my blessing
In this world of unsurety
From an ever changing life
You remain steady but not staid
The confidence of hope
Cloaks me in comfort
And I will rest easy
And i will rise well
Because I know that
I will remain yours
Until the tide does not retur

The Ink

My hands have been wrinkled with time
It's tough to hold onto truth
So i paint it on my mind and on my arms
Words, images, pictures and memories
The weight is heavy across my shoulders
But that is Your way, to keep me focused
To my task of repetition and salve
Sketches of hearts in indigo, ochre, dirt
Smoke fills my sacred space
Scents of myrrh and fragrant incense
Reminding me of my needs nor wants
Apart from your grace

My story is one of fingers and wrists
Clutched in embraces cold and barren
Of essential smoothness flowing
From lips and across tongues
And the most secret inward places
That only You can see, when i bow
Forehead to the stone tablets
Laws unmitigated by science or physics
Knees bent and ankles straightened
Elbows taunt into unfeeling
my eyes and the corner of my mouth
Silvery liquid dried at the edges
A well pumped and abandoned
In a dry place
Words that can only be whispered
For the lack of a perceived answer
So i wait on Your breath
To smooth back the edges

i paint in words unknown to me
It coils across my limbs
And creeps inside my heart
i have shaved my head for more space
Palms to palms my entreaties
Gather together in tongues not my own
Ancient and not heard aloud
For it is oft misunderstood
This longing for peace
A need for contentment
To return to the rib from which i came

And i am here before you
Before the breaking of one fast
And the beginning of another
Forgive me for my story
Though it is a testament
Not to my hopelessness
But to Your faithfulness
Grant ease to this stained soul

Alicja Maria Kuberska

Alicja Maria Kuberska

Alicja Maria Kuberska – awarded Polish poetess, novelist, journalist, editor.

She is a member of the Polish Writers Associations in Warsaw, Poland and IWA Bogdani, Albania. She is also a member of directors' board of Soflay Literature Foundation, Our Poetry Archive (India) and Cultural Ambassador for Poland (Inner Child Press, USA)

Her poems have been published in numerous anthologies and magazines in : Poland, Czech Republic, Slovakia, Hungary,Ukraina, Belgium, Bulgaria, Albania, Spain, the UK, Italy, the USA, Canada, the UK, Argentina, Chile, Peru, Israel, Turkey, India, Uzbekistan, South Korea, Taiwan, China, Australia, South Africa, Zambia, Nigeria

She received two medals - the Nosside UNESCO Competition in Italy (2015) and European Academy of Science Arts and Letters in France (2017). Ahe also received a reward of international literary competition in Italy „ Tra le parole e 'elfinito" (2018). She was announced a poet of the 2017 year by Soflay Literature Foundation (2018).She also received : Bolesław Prus Prize Poland (2019), Culture Animator Poland (2019) and first prize Premio Internazionale di Poesia Poseidonia- Paestrum Italy (2019).

Poems on The Lake Ohrid

Three shades of blue – mists, mountains and sky
fell softly into the water in a wide cascade.
The fishing boats were lying lazily
on the yellow sand of a nearby beach
- gazing at golden reflections glistening
on the smooth surface of the lake

It was a beautiful day - full of sunshine and love
There were roses and the wind hid in the flowers,
to listen to the silence interrupted
with the carefree laughter of playing children.
The old people sat down on the park benches
- they were similar to birds tired after a long flight

In the odeon, as in ancient times,
the subtle music of the words sounded.
Here we were, the wanderers from distant lands
- we spoke with all the languages of the world
and we felt the common speech of poetry

The differences are gone.
In our veins,
in the same rhythm drops of blood throbbed,
calmness settled in our minds.
Against the world, full of wars and hatred,
we built a new tower of Babel
to climb above the walls and touch the azure sky.

Festival of poetry, North Macedonia 2021

Infinity

I am a fragment of light enclosed in matter,
A word brought to life,
A memory inscribed in my genes.
Each day I climb, like a vine,
Along the branches of the tree of knowledge
Of good and evil —
Advancing step by step.
I possess free will.
I can choose the sunlit path or the shaded one,
Bear fruits that are sweet or bitter.
I am grateful for the gift of life and awareness.
With hope, I look toward the future,
Journeying toward infinity.

Fulfilment

With thought, I shape reality,
Weaving events on a loom of dreams.
I speak the words — and they gain power.
Fate has given, and fate has stolen.
It planted doubt within my mind
— Whispered that things could have been better.
And yet, I surrendered to what came,
— I am where I am meant to be,
And I do not curse destiny.
I have learned to rejoice and laugh,
To speak with leaves and birds,
To play with each fleeting moment and word.

Jackie Davis Allen

Jackie Davis Allen, otherwise known as Jacqueline D. Allen or Jackie Allen, grew up in the Cumberland Mountains of Appalachia. As the next eldest daughter of a coal miner father and a stay at home mother, she was the first in her family to attend and graduate from college. Her siblings, in their own right, are accomplished, though she is the only one, to date, that has discovered the gift of writing.

Graduating from Radford University, with a Bachelor's of Science degree in Early Education, she taught in both public and private schools. For over a decade she taught private art classes to children both in her home and at a local Art and Framing Shop where she also sold her original soft sculptured Victorian dolls and original christening gowns.

She resides in northern Virginia with her husband, taking much needed get-aways to their mountain home near the Blue Ridge Mountains, a place that evokes memories of days spent growing up in the Appalachian Mountains.

A lover of hats, she has worn many. Following marriage to her college sweetheart, and as wife, mother, grandmother, teacher, tutor, artist, writer, poet and crafter, she is a lover of art and antiques, surrounding herself, always, with books, seeking to learn more.

In 2015 she authored *Looking for Rainbows, Poetry, Prose and Art*, and in 2017, *Dark Side of the Moon*. Both books of mostly narrative poetry were published by Inner Child Press and were edited by hulya n. yilmaz in 2019, *No Illusions. Through the Looking Glass*, which was nominated to be considered for a Pulitzer Prize by the publisher and editor of Inner Child Press, ltd.

http://www.innerchildpress.com/jackie-davis-allen.php
jackiedavisallen.com

Connections

My mother-in-law: she obtained
Her Master's Degree, with honors.
The same year that I received
My BS degree, in Early Education.

Despite, the connection,
Both of us loving her son,
When it came to letter writing,
I was intimidated by her expertise.

"I'm not reading with red pen.
We just want to hear from you."
This coming from one with
A column in a local newspaper.

It continued on, like that, for a time,
Until I felt more comfortable.
Time passed, our letters continuing
Back and forth through the mail.

Along, with the once a week, phone call.
Too much a strain on our budget
For any more-frequent interactions.
Cell phones, internet still in the future.

Years later, both knees, a doctor's
Diagnosis: surgery and bilateral
Replacement. Both find a date
On my to-do calendar. But when?

"After the Steeplechase Race
In May. A request, please.
Will you replace both knees
At the same time?"

He agrees. I facetiously, almost,
Ask my surgeon to replace my knees
With ones to increase my height, I'm
Little more than five feet tall.

He said, "Impossible. He leaves.
I'll be back in a moment or so."
He slipped inside an adjacent cubicle.
I imagine it similar to mine.

Between thin walls, separating
Our examining rooms, I hear
A male voice, a patient. Pleading.
"Do mine on the same day, like hers".

I hear, "You don't understand.
She can handle it. You can't. "
This from his having performed
Two previous surgeries on me.

How interesting it is to discover,
That from serendipity, from pain,
The door can open to so much more
To a greater fulfillment of self.

And, the healing of lingering feelings
Within, awaiting opportunity,
As from revealed acknowledgment,
Discovery, reason, excuse. Need.

Healing well, pain not yet dissipated,
Able to dance, walk, but with winter
Coming, how was I to get up, were I to fall?
I was unwilling to be held hostage.

A Writing Workshop was offered, free
Of charge. All I had to do was to register.
But I waited, until the last minute. Not

Because it was too difficult to drive.

Rather, because, being honest
With myself, I felt uneasy.
Uncomfortable at the thought
Of revealing too much of myself.

Or, able to withstand the scrutiny.
Something akin to standing naked
In front of my peers. I hobbled down
The steps, registration accepted.

I hesitated. There's time enough
To turn around, to leave; I tell myself.
Yet a voice in my ear
Whispers, "Go on inside".

The connection between pain,
Physically, emotionally, even
Self-inflicted had opened up
New avenues to self awareness.

Today I am an author,
A writer, a published poet,
With three books to my credit.
Ten years, plus, as contributing poet

To The Year of the Poet magazine;
Four years of contributing poetry
to my church's monthly newsletter.
and, some international notoriety.
The Virginia Mountaineer,
my hometown newspaper,
Published an extensive article
About me and my writing.

My third book, was nominated
For a Pulitzer Prize, by my publisher.
Several of my poems were
Nominated for a Pushcart Prize.

A friend, Dr. John T Martin
Has beautifully composed music
For piano, and or guitar,
To accompany one of my poems.

Listening, yielding to heart's hope
Fulfills my deepest creative need.
It allows me to share the gifts
With which I have been blessed.

Fulfillment

Opening up the wellspring

Wherein lies the untapped,

The risk outweighs
Any thought of rejection.

Only thoughts

Of heart and mind's expression

Of thankfulness expressed
For the thirst quenched.

And for the fulfillment found there.

Hope

As long as health's wealth lasts,

As long as lungs breathe, and

As long as my pen can move

Or my finger can tap,

May the words that flow out

From my pen, find approval

With the One who instilled

In me the gift of poetry.

,

Jackie Davis Allen

Tzemin
Ition
Tsai

Dr. Tzemin Ition Tsai comes from the Republic of China(Taiwan). In addition to being a professor of literature at a university, he is more committed to writing poems, novels, and proses. He is also an editor of "Reading, Writing and Teaching" academic text, an International editor of "Contemporary dialogues" literary periodical in Macedonia, and Vice-Chairman of the International Jury of the SAHITTO INTERNATIONAL AWARD in Bangladesh, and a columnist for "Chinese Language Monthly" in Taiwan.

In a wide range of literary creations, he is particularly fond of interesting stories or novels, and writing articles or poems about the feelings of nature and human beings. He has won many national literary awards. His literary works have been anthologized and published in books, journals, and newspapers in more than 55 countries and have been translated into more than 24 languages.

Ode to the Bud of Spring

On the Loess Plateau, the snow lies heavy this year.
Old Zhang's wheat, last autumn, lay unsown.
From the village loudspeaker, echoes call for reforestation;
his son has long since moved to the city.
Yet in the dead of winter, he carves the frost, sowing again.
His wife sighs with a life-worn breath "Three decades of toil?"
He scratches his head, saying nothing aloud,
but softly within: "Last night, I dreamed of spring."

The seeds beneath snow are cold as hammered iron.
Each dawn, he walks the field,
as one waiting for a letter forever delayed.
Come March, the wind softens, and beside the field,
a mulberry tree unfurls the tiniest shoot.
Zhang opens his lips and laughs: "Ah, spring, you've
chosen to believe me once more."

Hope is not the art of waiting, but of faith.
Faith that a flicker will one day brush past snow and stir the soil.
Faith that, within one's heart,
a sliver of green may still be planted, unsurrendered.
Amid crumbling walls and wintry winds,
there sleeps one thought, not yet dead.

Night-Blooming Accord

At the bean curd stall west of town, she's sold unsweetened syrup for thirty years,
Each night, before shuttering the shop, she nods to the empty chair.
Has he appeared today?
She asks the wind, though truly, she means the husband who never returned.

In youth, he chased a northern dream,
And sent back, in the end, a single lamp.
She could not bring herself to light it.
It sleeps now in the drawer, the way hope slumbers in silence.
Each day, unchanged: she feeds the cat, stirs the broth, replaces the curtain's fade,
Sometimes folding her hands before the temple's Guanyin,
And within that hush, wonders:
Was this life of mine not lived in vain?

That evening, spring still cold, a child came for a bowl of tofu,
And as she served it, something glimmered inside.
The unopened lamp, glowing softly in the heart's far chamber.
Fulfillment was not in his return,
But in her long-awaited accord with memory itself.
There are flowers of the soul that bloom
Only in nights where no eye lingers.
To be replete in spirit
Is to desire, quietly, a blossom that opens in shadow.

The Loom of Hearts

At the lane's southern end, where the opera stage gathers
dust,
Two cups of tea cool untouched in twilight hush.
She comes from the alley of willows,
Cradling a piece of torn cloth.
He, beneath the window, mends a fishing net,
His brows stitched with the silence of years.

"This eye of the needle," she says, "cannot mend all that
was unsaid."
She smiles. He answers not,
Yet in the same small tear,
Glimpse the flicker of lives long passed.

It is not love, not longing,
But something older, a recognition born before names.
At the loose thread of an old sleeve,
Both pause,
The forgotten warmth of frayed fabric
Holding the unfinished rings of their shared time.

If souls could be woven,
They would be like a wind-drawn curtain's shadow,
Two life threads drawn tight on the same spindle,
Spinning a poem in the clamor of the marketplace.
And there they sit, unmoved,
Listening to their hearts weaving dreams.

They weave not for passion, but for the harmony of souls.
Each stitch a fated meeting, each thread a silent destiny.

Noreen Snyder

Noreen Snyder

Noreen Ann Snyder has been writing since she was a teenager. She writes a variety of different topics. Her favorite poetic forms are Sonnets, Blitz, Haiku, Tanka, and Free Verse. She always learning different poetic forms.

Noreen Ann Snyder is a poet, writer, and an author of five books, (four books are co-authored with her late husband, Garry A. Snyder.) Her poetry is in several Inner Child Press Anthologies. She is the founder ofThe Poetry Club on Facebook.

Hope

I look forward to the future
with positive attitudes,
hopes, and dreams.
You're never too old or
too young to live your dreams...
new dreams, old dreams.

My new dream is to
be the best I can be as
a Kick streamer
putting poetry out there.

My old dreams are to keep on
writing poetry,
learning more poetic forms,
and publishing more poetry books.

Yes, my hope for the future
will be better
for God is here with me
leading me on.

Warm Summer Mornings

It's one of these
warm, summer mornings
I just want
to play, walk, dance
in the rain
while thinking of you,
My Sweetheart.
I just want
to reach to the sky
pulling you down
here with me
no worries in the world
Just listen to the orchestra!
It must be our angels!
Oh, isn't this romantic?
Play, walk, and dance
in the rain with you.

Memories: Dancing With You

Dancing with you
like leaves falling
slowly from the branch
spinning, shaking, twisting,

just having fun.
Oh, if only, if only we had
another chance to do it again
but now it's too late.
I still have these memories.
It will never fade away.
No one can take it away
not even Death.

Elizabeth E. Castillo

Elizabeth Esguerra Castillo

Elizabeth Esguerra Castillo is a multi-awarded and an Internationally-Published Contemporary Author/Poet and a Professional Writer / Creative Writer / Feature Writer / Journalist / Travel Writer from the Philippines. She has 2 published books, "Seasons of Emotions" (UK) and "Inner Reflections of the Muse", (USA). Elizabeth is also a co-author to more than 60 international anthologies in the USA, Canada, UK, Romania, India. She is a Contributing Editor of Inner Child Magazine, USA and an Advisory Board Member of Reflection Magazine, an international literary magazine. She is a member of the American Authors Association (AAA) and PEN International.

Web links:

Facebook Fan Page

https://free.facebook.com/ElizabethEsguerraCastillo

Google Plus

https://plus.google.com/u/0/+ElizabethCastillo

Entwined Souls

A whisper soft, a silent plea,
A yearning deep, eternally.
A thread of light, a fragile grace,
A bond that time cannot erase.

Across the miles, a whispered name,
A shared experience, a kindred flame.
A mirrored soul, a heart's embrace,
A symphony of love and space.

Through laughter shared and tears that fall,
A tapestry of moments, standing tall.
A connection forged in gentle hand,
A sacred trust, throughout the land.

From distant shores to skies so high,
A whispered word, beneath the sky.
A bond that binds, a love profound,
A connection, deeply understood and sound.

In every touch, a whispered vow,
A silent promise, ever now.
A heart entwined, a soul's delight,
A connection burning ever bright.

Purpose

A tapestry woven, thread by thread of dreams,
Where whispered hopes in silent shadows gleam.
A journey's start, a path yet to unfold,
A story whispered, yet to be grown old.

From fragile seedlings, reaching for the sun,
A blossoming flower, brightly, bravely spun.
Each tiny petal, a moment cherished deep,
A silent promise, secrets softly keep.

The heart's soft pulse, a rhythm strong and true,
A melody of moments, old and new.
With every step, a lesson learned with grace,
A gentle whisper, finding its own place.

Through trials faced, and burdens gently borne,
A strength discovered, a spirit newly born.
The soul takes flight, on wings of hopeful might,
And finds its haven, bathed in golden light.

Guiding Star

A fragile whisper, soft and low,
A flicker caught in shadows' flow,
A seed of yearning, deep and true,
Hope's gentle dawn, a vibrant hue.

Through darkest nights, it softly sighs,
A guiding star within the skies,
A whispered promise, faint and clear,
A beacon burning, banishing fear.

Though storms may rage, and winds may blow,
And shadows lengthen, to and fro,
Hope's steady flame, a constant light,
Igniting embers, burning bright.

A whispered prayer, a hopeful plea,
A whispered dream, for you and me,
In moments fractured, hearts in pain,
Hope's gentle touch, a soothing rain.

A whispered word, a tender touch,
A whispered promise, held so much,
A whispered hope, that blossoms forth,
A symphony of joy and worth.

For in the depths, where darkness hides,
A spark of hope, forever glides,
A steadfast faith, a guiding hand,
To heal the wounds, across the land.

So let us hold, this precious thing,
This fragile flower, on hopeful wing,
For in its grace, and gentle might,
Hope's radiant dawn, forever bright.

Mutawaf Shaheed

Mutawaf Shaheed

C. E. Shy has been writing since the seventh grade. He continued writing through high school, until he became more involved in sports. After his graduation, he worked at the White Motors Company where he wrote for the company's newspaper. He started a column called: "The Poet's Corner." That was his first published work.

www.innerchildpress.com/c-e-shy.php

While We Can

Hey grandson walk come with
me while we can, talk with me
while you can.

I may be able to point out some
things you don't see. I can tell
you some stuff you don't understand.

I will give you some knowledge
that will put out front of the
crowd.

I'll show a way you can side step
trouble and stay   out of jail, to
keep your parents from posting
a bail.

I know right now you think you
know. If you take this walk with
me, you'll see you don't.

If you apply what I teach, you may
survive. Asking your friends, don't
bother, until they take a walk with
their grandfather.

You Got A Deal

There was hand stitched wit on his
upper lip, the words were as sharp
as shards.

All the stones were over turned so
there was nothing one could hide.
Quick witted opponents, typhooned!

Their speech was breached before
they spoke. Ambushed thoughts lay
along- side abandoned minds.

His ear hears their minds squeak, even
as the things they think begin to
form.

It was the status quo that screwed
them. Hand-picked tricks packed
their eyes with lies.

Now, flies won't leave them alone.
Mass mental incarceration, that was
planned for others, has them doing
the time.

The TV is the warden. It was too late
to escape a programed fate. That
paradigm wasn't worth one nickel.

They 're, now enjoying going along
for the ride.

Trane Ride

I rode the Trane into the Deen.
I left the stains where I found them.

I located the other words that were
hidden in plain sight.

No more mental fetters to bind me.
I was unaccustomed to that kind of piece
of mindlessness.

It was a new rush. Being lifted from the
madness that surrounded me. Cool!

There was an honor I never knew.
I was un-deluded by a knowledge that
couldn't be disputed.

No substitution for what's real.
Well, that's my overview of a
personal shared opinion.

hülya
n.
yılmaz

Liberal Arts Professor Emerita, hülya n. yılmaz [sic] is Co-Chair and Director of Editing Services at Inner Child Press International, a published author, ghostwriter, and translator (EN, DE, and TU; in any direction). Her literary contributions appeared in a large number of national and international anthologies.

hülya writes creatively to attain and nourish a comprehensive awareness for and development of our humanity.

hülya n. yılmaz, a traveler on the journey called "life" . . .

Writing Web Site
https://hulyanyilmaz.com/

Editing Web Site
https://hulyasfreelancing.com

Rowing Against the Current

Holding a pail with large holes in it
In a boat on a stormy sea,
Trying in vain to dump the water
Where it belongs.

No land in sight.
Once again,
Facing a plight
Of overwhelming proportions.

Arms are limp now.
Lungs, out of breath.
Sleep deprivation settles in.
Eyelids sit down heavily onto their seat.

Hallucination?
No, no! There IS a light in the distance!
Must make it there. Must make it there.
Hoping against hope is going nowhere!

A Phone Call

How many of them have I skipped?
Calling a loved one simply to say, "Hello!"
Not much of an effort!

Remembering the immense joy I felt
When a beloved gave me a phone call
Out of the blue.

The smile on my face would linger.
Yet, I have failed to give the same gift
To precious others.

A phone call . . .
Was that too much to ask?

promises

fulfill a promise

you have made to anyone

don't neglect yourself

Teresa E. Gallion

Teresa E. Gallion is a seeker on a journey to work on unfolding spiritually in this present lifetime. Writing is a spiritual exercise for Teresa. Her passions are traveling the world and hiking the mountain and desert landscapes of the western United States. Her journeys into nature are nurtured by the Sufi poets Rumi and Hafiz. The land is sacred ground and her spiritual temple where she goes for quiet reflection and contemplation. She has published five books: Walking Sacred Ground, Contemplation in the High Desert, Chasing Light, a finalist in the 2013 New Mexico/Arizona Book Awards, Scent of Love, a finalist in the 2021 New Mexico/Arizona Book Awards and Come Egypt in 2024. She has two CDs, *On the Wings of the Wind* and *Poems from Chasing Light*. Her work has appeared in numerous journals and anthologies.

Website: http://teresagallion.yolasite.com/

Links to Connection

We embrace moments.
Bound to time and memories stored.
The thought of what stands behind us
becomes our connection to earth.

Words collide and ears hear
voices from the past.
We accept and reject things we hear.
Everything is a lesson
binding us to time and space.

Everlasting bonds are tied
to our shared experiences.
We can reject moment by moment.
The thin veil of connection
is never cut loose.

It lingers in our dreams.
Scratches us in our sleep.
Follows us on every walk.
Teases us with every breath we take.

The eyes do not deceive
if we dare to look.
Connection always rides the waves.
It lands gentle or rough dependent
on where you stand in the moment.

Cup of Contentment

Morning light stretches at dawn.
Fills me with gratitude
for this exhale from my lungs.

No words may prescribe meaning
to the fullness that embraces the soul
with the first breath of the day.

That first sip of coffee
titillates the lips.
Fills the heart with ecstatic trembles.

Whispers in the breeze
sound like a call to prayer
to bend your knees in gratefulness.

The light stream rubs the ears
with a delicate message.
Open your arms to love.

I will not tell
if you do not tell.
Joyfulness is a full cup of love.

Hope Is

Hope is a whisper
that massages the earlobes.
A resilient tease,
like a gentle breeze.

Hope is a scent
that lingers in your nose.
Tickling the hair follicles
that defend your airways.

Hope is a taste
that hangs out on your tongue.
Always ready to motivate you
with an unbroken song.

Hope is a vision
connected to your brainwaves.
Waiting for you to look
deep within your soul.

Hope is a touch
that binds you to commit
to the universal truth.
Never, ever give up.

Hope is a resistance move
that shows courage
in daring steps
with each inhaled breath.

Ashok
K.
Bhargava

Ashok Bhargava is a poet, writer, inspirational speaker and a literary consultant. He has attended poetry conferences in Italy, Turkey, India and Philippines. His latest book "Riding the Tide" about his battle with cancer has been translated and published in Arabic, Hindi, Telugu and Bengali languages. He is a contributing writer to several anthologies worldwide including World Poetry Almanac 2014. He has been published in numerous print and online magazines.

Ashok has won many accolades including Poet Ambassador to Japan, Kalidasa International award, World Poetry Lifetime Achievement award, Writers Beyond Borders Peace award and Tapsilog Leadership award for his community involvement. He is founder of Writers International Network Canada Society to discover, nourish, recognize and celebrate writers, poets and artists and to assist them to network with the community at large. He is the author of eight books of poetry and one anthology. He is Artist-in-Residence at Moberly Arts & Cultural Centre and also co-edits the literary section of The Link Newspaper.

Fulfillment

"while the truth has many forms, love stands apart."

I compose poems
like marigold flowers
yellow, gold, pastel and maroon
carefully pierced and
threaded
into a garland of colorful harmony
placed on your lap
to evoke monsoon dreams.

Words drop
like rain
to inflame
craving for you.

I am waiting
to be loved
to be fulfilled.

Hope

Hope is a seed that lays in darkness
beneath the dirt
not fully conceived
pulling gently toward the light.

Hope must not be diminished
by fate or man
kept alive
through the darkness of the night.

Bodies decay with the passage of time
yours and mine.
Just hope and hush, nothing remains
all turns into the dust.

Connection

It's not rare
for a moment
to lay in eternity.

Time always
runs out
for the hide-and-seek sun.

Come out and connect
with beauty of nature
waiting to be noticed.

A giant
floating in the western sky
painting you pink with glee.
Windows opened
letting soft breeze in
Kissing you in bliss.

Caroline 'Ceri Naz' Nazareno Gabis

Caroline 'Ceri' Nazareno-Gabis

Caroline 'Ceri Naz' Nazareno-Gabis, author of Velvet Passions of Calibrated Quarks, World Poetry Canada International Director to Philippines is a multi-awarded poet, editor, journalist, educator, peace and women's advocate. She believes that learning other's language and culture is a doorway to wisdom.

Among her poetic belts include **Gabrielle Galloni Memorial Panorama International Youth Award** 2022, Panorama Youth Literary Awards 2020, 7th Prize Winner in the 19th, 20th and 21st Italian Award of Literary Festival; Writers International Network-Canada ''Amazing Poet 2015'', The Frang Bardhi Literary Prize 2014 (Albania), Poet Journalist Award 2014 (Tuzla, Istanbul, Turkey) and World Poetry Empowered Poet 2013 (Vancouver, Canada). She's a featured member of Association of Women's Rights and Development (AWID), The Poetry Posse, Galaktika Poetike, Asia Pacific Writers and Translators (APWT), Axlepino and Anacbanua. Her poetry and children's stories have been featured in different anthologies and magazines worldwide.

Links to her works:

http://panitikan.ph/2018/03/30/caroline-nazareno-gabis/

https://apwriters.org/author/ceri_naz/

http://www.aveviajera.org/nacionesunidasdelasletras/id1181.html

boketto
(gazing vacantly at a distance)

Dear mind,
i can feel you,
as moments blend
into an endless firmament,
eyes escape weightless,
dreams float unfolding,
like a tumbleweed,
thoughts dissolve
in falling waters,
nexus of nature,
interconnected
in my veins,
i am suddenly lost,
but i exist.

Quotidian

Day by day
You're part of the puzzle,
that's a routine being fulfilled,
existence in every way
the one that got away!
your masterplan bears numbers,
engraved totems
and codes of humanity,
like waking up for another day,
is a fulfillment
of a dream,
that never wane.

The Distance Nearest to Hope

Storms circling in the Pacific,
People fear of the flood and of soil erosion,
When the strong winds strike all roofs and fall in the
ground,
It gives distance of losing a home,
When the home becomes waterworld,
The dreams vanish,
but calling it home gives foundation,
of love, of strength and of resilience,
People extend hands
to let you feel,
The Distance of Moving forward is still there,
The more empowered soul you become,
Rising beyond the nature's call,
Rising above the floodwaters and trip for tomorrow and
after,
 Calamities end through the colors of the arising sun,
I look at the nearest distance,
The hope of unstoppable force.

Swapna Behera

Swapna Behera is a trilingual poet, translator, environmentalist, editor from India and author of seven books of different genres including one on children's literature on Environment. She is the recipient of International UGADI AWARD 2019, honoured from Gujurat Sahitya Akademi 2022, 2021 International Poesis Award of Honor as Jury, Pentasi B World Fellow Poet, Honoured Poet of India from Seychelles Government and International awards from Algeria, Morocco, Kajhakhstan, modern Arabic Literary Renaissance of Egypt, International Arts Council Argentina etc. Her stories, poems, articles are published in many International and National magazines and ezines. Her poem A NIGHT IN THE REFUGEE CAMP is translated into 67 languages. She has received over 60 National and International Awards. At present she is the Cultural Ambassador for India and South Asia of Inner Child and the life member of Odisha Environmental Society

Email
swapna.behera@gmail.com

Web Site
http://swapnabehera.in/

The Wings Of Hope
Hope is the last thing ever lost

is hope a Lazarus syndrome?
even if the heartbeat stops for sometimes
 a sudden unexpected heartbeat brings life even after the
death
hope always winks at the horizon
it has many forms,
an open road, a radiant page
where a new story can be written
it is a lost and found ring
that always promises a new commitment
a new document to build a new civilization
hope heals, feels the vibration to march
fills the era with zeal
to end all ordeal
a beam of light at the end of a tunnel
hope sings near the cradle or coffin
yes, hope is the anthem of victory over fear
a butterfly on the mast of a submarine

Fulfillment

I just wanted to be a queen
with the crown on my head
yes, I am a farmer's daughter
can you see the basket of corns on my head
I grow food
my sweat and blood are crowned
the bright sunshine in my courtyard;
plants in the periphery
no traffic sound or dust pollution
I get oxygen, free water of the spring
people surrounded by sprinkle the values
the granny speaks of the chronicles
the soul starts with a haiku and ends with a sonnet
liberation ends all traumas
let there be an architect
who can build and paint the fragrances of contentment
grass has a dream, The Sun has a dream too
let our hands spread and stretch to both ends
yes, I hereby declare I am happy
 my soul is fulfilled with peace and love
mother nature is holding my hand
so why should I cry?
allow me to smile

Connection

tear of one is tear of all
vowels and consonants are spread
only the alphabets are different
you have porridge in dinner
I have roti
but hunger is the common spice in our plates
the haves and have-nots strive
as survival is the issue
sometimes stories swirl hurricanes
battles lead to wars
ego crosses boundaries to be the superego
blasphemy gives birth to weapons
always the mother waits
at times quantum physics crawls;
the journey starts from a dot
 to reach existentialism

Albert 'Infinite' Carrasco

Albert 'Infinite' Carassco

Albert "Infinite The Poet" Carrasco is an urban poet, mentor and public speaker.

Albert believes his experience of growing up in poverty, dealing with drugs and witnessing murder over and over were lessons learnt, in order to gain knowledge to teach. Albert's harsh reality and honesty is a powerfully packed punch delivered through rhyme. Infinite grew up in the east part of the Bronx and still resides there, so he knows many young men will follow the same dark path he followed looking for change. The life of crime should never be an option to being poor but it is, very often.

Infinite poetry @lulu.com

Alcarrasco2 on YouTube

Infinite the poet on reverbnation

Infinite Poetry

www.lulu.com/us/en/shop/al-infinite-carrasco/infinite-poetry/paperback/product-21040240.html

www.innerchildpress.com/albert-carrasco

Hope

Hope is the one thing in life that I'll never give up. Hope gave me a reason to look forward to another day. No matter how hard life was to me, I would just pray for the best while expecting the worst. There were always more bad times than good times, so the norm to me was chaos and misery. I knew the sun would come out tomorrow before the Little Orphan Annie, it just took many tomorrows before the dark cloud left and life got sunny. I got a chance to eat when I was hungry, I got a place to sleep with a permanent roof over me and my family, we finally got the opportunity to live contentedly without the assistance of the government for food, clothing, and shelter. That's what I call fulfillment. We broke the chains of poverty that was passed on for years and years from parents to children as an unwanted tradition; hope was how we ended monetary oppression. Now I pass down hope from generation to generation with words of encouragement and motivation. I share my experience with trial and tribulation with the world to show that giving up should never be an option.

Kimberly Burnham

Kimberly Burnham

A brain health expert (PhD in Integrative Medicine) and award-winning poet, Kimberly Burnham lives with her wife and family in Spokane, Washington. Kim speaks extensively on peace, brain health, and *"Awakenings: Peace Dictionary, Language and the Mind, a Daily Brain Health Program."* She recently published *"Heschel and King Marching to Montgomery A Jewish Guide to Judeo-Tamarian Imagery."* Currently work includes *"Call and Response To Maya Stein an Anthology of Wild Writing"* and a how-to non-fiction book, *"Using Ekphrastic Fiction Writing and Poetry to Create Interest and Promote Artists, Writers, and Poets."*

Follow her at https://amzn.to/4fcWnRB

Let Them

Let the birds sing you awake
not with chaos, but with wonder
the morning light already loosening
the last dark threads of night

Let the warmth come
a silk blanket spreading over your skin
as if the world has begun again
invites you to begin
with hope and light

Let the roads' curve winding beneath
tall tunnels of trees overhead
their green hands blessing your lungs
a natural embrace supportiung you

Let the narrow bridges carry you
not just across rivers and avenues
but across quiet worries
between one breath and another

Let the city pause in its rush
engines idling, people waiting
each one with a reason
a hope, a yearning
trying to arrive by nine am
at something that matters
meaningful work, a child's game,
a torah study or prayer

Let them speak
telling you why
they cannot understand
listen
not because they are right

but because listening stretches
the muscles of the heart
and sometimes through a doorway
love walks in

Let them talk
the ones who scowl at difference
who carry sharp metal
in their voices

Let them pass by
because there are also those who smile
like a lighthouse on your path
who remember your name
who offer you back
wholeness and peace

Let dogs shed on your black pants
your clean shirt.
leaping, howling and loving you
with their entire body
without needing a reason

Let them heal
however they must
let them name their pain
in languages you don't speak
hold beliefs
like magical pebbles in their pockets
for who among us has ever known
every step of the whole path

Let creativity come
as rain does
not craving permission
from the ground
drenching you
wild and soft

carving paths
toward connection
toward the world
we still hope to make

Let it all be
Let them
Let us

Where I Am From

I am from pioneers
not the shouting boasting kinds
but the quiet ones who walked
toward an open sky
seeking a place where seeds take root
and water runs clean

We know how to listen
to the rhythm of the earth
how to dig deep
for something that feeds
body and soul

I am from street corners and libraries,
from hands blistered by work
and minds bent over books
from sweat, from ink,
from words that mean survival
and also, give meaning

I come from the mountain
its green summer back
giving way to gold
then snowy white

I have stood where the air is thin
and the sky feels closer than the tree tops
but I am also of the sea
where starfish linger in tidal pools
and starlight spills on midnight waves
where every rise and fall
is a lesson in letting go and moving forward
with more knowledge and less stuff
more relationships and love

I am also from the place
where deserts meet water
the in between places
of strength and challenges
where heat holds silence

I am from artists
from color that dares to be bigger than life
from shapes that don't quite belong
but insist on being seen
from the square peg and the round hole
from the ones who say

Try again
try differently
see what beauty
can be made
telling us something new
about the space
about how we each can fit and
how sometimes we have to be
more creative
when nothing fits
until you reimagine
the space

This is where I am from
soil and salt
canvas and questions
from every place
that asked something of me
and gives back a piece of myself
in return

With the Certainty of the Tides

"With the certainty of the tides"
Maya Angelou said it,
and something in me opened

I remembered beaches
in far-off lands
where the sun kissed the sea
with no apology
where I stood
tall and sun-warmed
sand clinging to my feet
as the waves
whispered their ancient rhythm

In Hawaii,
just steps from college
I learned the tides by heart
I watched starfish move across coral
anemones folding in like secret caves
at low tide waiting for the sea
to rise again

I believed then
that love would always return
a tide
a rhythm
a certainty

Now
after a fight
words flung like shells
sharp and breaking

I sit in a quiet forest waiting
for her voice

soft again
for the air to clear
for the tide of love
to rise and wash over us
make smooth the broken places

Still
I listen for the tide
I hope
for the swell
because if love is anything
it is not always certain
it is not always soft
but it is
like the tide
returning
a rhythm
we remember
even when the shoreline
is dry

Eliza Segiet

Eliza Segiet

Eliza Segiet graduated with a Master's Degree in Philosophy at Jagiellonian University.

Received *Global Literature Guardian Award* – from Motivational Strips, World Nations Writers Union and Union Hispanomundial De Escritores (UHE) 2018.

Nominated for the Pushcart Prize 2019, 2021.

Laureate *Naji Naaman Literary Prize 2020,*

International Award Paragon of Hope (2020),

World Award 2020 *Cesar Vallejo* for Literary Excellence. Laureate of the Special Jury *Sahitto International Award* 2021, World Award *Premiul Fănuş Neagu* 2021.

Finalist *Golden Aster Book* World Literary Prize 2020, *Mili Dueli* 2022, Voci nel deserto 2022.

At the international Festival of Poetry CAMPIONATO MONDIALE DI POESIA (2021/2022) she won the title of vice-champion of the world.

Award BHARAT RATNA RABINDRANATH TAGORE INTERNATIONAL AWARD (2022).

Award - *World Poets Association* (2023).

Laureate Between words and infinity *"International Literary Award (2023).*

Plans

For a moment, he realized
that this journey,
this exhausting flight, was his
– to live or not to live.
Gazing at the clouds,
looking down below,
he was scared. He was scared as hell!

When he saw the snow-covered hills,
his unspoken thoughts
whispered
that nothing bad would happen.
He was not alone.
All those
who, at the same time, in the same place,
were – like him –
torn between Shakespeare's
– *to be or not to be.*
They too had fear,
but they had plans as well.

Translated by Dorota Stępińska

Voices

It did happen!
I am who I wanted to be.
A doctor – oh, how it sounds!
Yet, is it enough
to understand a person?

I have one more goal,
I will do it for myself
and for my patients.
Let philosophy
be the trampoline
to delve into their
and my own psyche.
This is it!
I will devote my time
to
– good,
– health,
– understanding.

To explore the unexplorable,
will be an attempt at a positive
uplifting of
– actions,
– words,
– thoughts.

A return
to a tranquil world.
A world free of
contrived voices.

Translated by Dorota Stępińska

Fame

She always knew
that she would do
what no one had managed before.
She wanted to gain fame and money.
She chose sports.
She trained all day,
exhausted, fell asleep in the evenings
only to do it all over again next morning.

Hoping that in another field
she might achieve something,
she kept wandering towards
attempts at uplifting herself.

Maybe fashion, beauty, health?
She changed her interests,
to become the person
who she was meant
to be
– the best mother of all.

A person has true value only when
they mean
– the whole world to another.

Translated by Dorota Stępińska

William S. Peters Sr.

William S. Peters, Sr.

Bill's writing career spans a period of well over 50 years. Being first Published in 1972, Bill has since went on to Author in excess of 50+ additional Volumes of Poetry, Short Stories, etc., expressing his thoughts on matters of the Heart, Spirit, Consciousness and Humanity. His primary focus is that of Love, Peace and Understanding!

Bill says . . .

I have always likened Life to that of a Garden. So, for me, Life is simply about the Seeds we Sow and Nourish. All things we "Think and Do", will "Be" Cause and eventually manifest itself to being an "Effect" within our own personal "Existences" and "Experiences" . . . whether it be Fruit, Flowers, Weeds or Barren Landscapes! Bill highly regards the Fruits of his Labor and wishes that everyone would thus go on to plant "Lovely" Seeds on "Good Ground" in their own Gardens of Life!

to connect with Bill, he is all things Inner Child

www.iaminnerchild.com

Personal Web Site

www.iamjustbill.com

I am the hope

i am the dream my Mother had
for a better world
that has yet to come true

i am the wish of my father
who sweated and bled
to provide a way
that my way
would be an easier one
for me, for you

to some degree it has
for i did not ever learn
to sacrifice my self
such as he did

i am the embodiment
of the aspirations of my ancestors
pooled in this collective consciousness
we call humanity . . .
are not we all ?

I offer my sacred seed to the Mother
that she may entomb it
in the Womb of Life
nurture it and bring forth to birth
the light of life . . . Love

for . . .

i am the hope

as are you !

Hope

It was a strange time, the strangest of times I have ever experienced in the entirety of my life. All the soldiers had laid down their guns, and they were smelted to make plows for our gardens that we may grow a natural food to feed ourselves healthily. Police Officers had shed their uniforms, tasers, clubs and weapons. People were milling around in the streets hugging each other. Of course, the children were still playing, faces adorned with unbound smiles with giggles and unrestrained laughter filling the air. There were many adults also pretending to be children, emulating an unbridled mirth and joy that has never before been witnessed on this earth to my limited knowledge.

Politicians of all levels had taken to the avenues and highways, marching through the cities, communities and neighborhoods, shaking hands, kissing babies and getting to know first hand the people they served. Solemn vows were being made from their hearts, and you could tell they were authentic by the apologetic tears running down their cheeks, tears of sorrow, tears of an awakening.

All the global despots and demons, had submitted themselves to the courts of righteousness, begging to be judged that they may begin the resurrection of their souls. Billionaires have given all their wealth away to feed and care for those in need. There was no longer such a thing as a 1% or 3% . . . there was only 100% WE, the People of Humanity.

Grocery Stores and Farms alike were open to the public. The objective was to feed the hungry. Hospitals and doctors required no paperwork nor signatures, they just went about the business of healing, as they were designed to do. Pastors, Ministers, Rabbis, Priests and Imams began again to service the soul as opposed to the habits of men and women alike and equally. We embraced our differences. The only colors we acknowledged were that of a yellow sun, the green of the plants and trees, the color of the petals of flowers, the blue skies, the diverse colors of our beautiful eyes, rainbows, th.at after the rain, and the variable beauty of our human pigmentation.

Builders were building, handymen were fixing, for all the people were of one accord . . . the betterment, health, safety and love . . . of all the people. Giving, sharing, loving and caring was its own reward.

Hope, it knows no limits save the limits we impose upon our possibilities.

Unspoken

There are words
Floating, hanging in the ether;
Questions, declarations
And idle conversations
That could have been voiced,
But have lost the opportunity,
For those who I wished
To offer them unto
Are no longer with us

At this juncture, this time
My heart, my soul is
Subjected to never be
Completely fulfilled
For I either
Had not the courage,
The time,
The inclination;
Or I was far too busy
Doing me
Instead of paying attention
To the things
That matter so much
Now

There are parents,
Loved ones,
Friends
And a myriad of others
For whom I could have
Picked a few flowers
And offered them
In a time of
Meaningfulness,
But yes,

As I said a bit before,
I was too busy

I now am destined
To speak these words
Into an unknow ether,
A void of non-understanding
Where I am facetiously
Hoping, praying'
They are heard
Along with my quest
For forgiveness
......
And my prayer is simply
That though I spoke not the words
At the most opportune times
In the past,
That they hear now
That which was
Once upon a time
Unspoken

August
2025
Featured Poets

~ * ~

Ivan Pozzoni

Ram Krishna Singh

Ibrahim Honjo

Kazimierz Burnat

i Fly

because ... said the Dreamer to the world. I Can

www.iamjustbill.com

Ivan Pozzoni

Ivan Pozzoni was born in Monza in 1976. Between 2007 and 2024, different versions of the books were published: Underground and Riserva Indiana, Versi Introversi, Mostri, Galata morente, Carmina non dant damen, Scarti di magazzino, Qui gli austriaci sono più severi dei Borboni, Cherchez the troika. et La malattia invettiva, Lame da rasoi, Il Guastatore, Patroclo non deve morire, and Kolektivne NSEAE. He wrote 150 volumes, wrote 1000 essays, founded an avant-garde movement (NéoN-avant-gardisme). His verses are translated into 25 languages. In 2024 he return to the Italian artistic world and melts the NSEAE Kolektivne (New socio/ethno/aesthetic anthropology).

Hotel Acapulco

Le mie mani, scarne, han continuato a batter testi,
trasformando in carta ogni voce di morto
che non abbia lasciato testamento,
dimenticando di curare
ciò che tutti definiscono il normale affare
d'ogni essere umano: ufficio, casa, famiglia,
l'ideale, insomma, di una vita regolare.

Abbandonata, nel lontano 2026, ogni difesa
d'un contratto a tempo indeterminato,
etichettato come squilibrato,
mi son rinchiuso nel centro di Milano,
Hotel Acapulco, albergo scalcinato,
chiamando a raccolta i sogni degli emarginati,
esaurendo i risparmi di una vita
nella pigione, in riviste e pasti risicati.

Quando i carabinieri faranno irruzione
nella stanza scrostata dell'Hotel Acapulco
e troveranno un altro morto senza testamento,
chi racconterà la storia, ordinaria,
d'un vecchio vissuto controvento?

Hotel Acapulco

My emaciated hands continued to write,
turning each voice of death into paper,
That he lefts no will,
forgetting to look after
what everyone defines as the normal business
of every human being: office, home, family,
the ideal, at last, of a regular life.

Abandoned, back in 2026, any defense
of a permanent contract,
labelled as unbalanced,
i'm locked up in the centre of Milan,
Hotel Acapulco, a decrepit hotel,
calling upon the dreams of the marginalized,
exhausting a lifetime's savings
in magazines and meagre meals.

When the Carabinieri burst
into the decrepit room of the Hotel Acapulco
and find yet another dead man without a will,
who will tell the ordinary story
of an old man who lived windbreak?

La Ballata Di Peggy E Pedro

La ballata di Peggy e Pedro è latrata dai *punkabbestia*
di Ponte Garibaldi, con un misto d'odio e disperazione,
insegnandoci, intimi nessi tra geometria ed amore,
ad amare come fossimo matematici circondati da cani
randagi.

Peggy eri ubriaca, stato d'animo normale,
nelle baraccopoli lungo l'alveo del Tevere,
e l'alcool, nelle sere d'Agosto, non riscalda,
obnubilando ogni senso in sogni annichilenti,
trasformando ogni frase biascicata in fucilate nella schiena
contro corazze disciolte dalla calura estiva.
Sdraiata sui bordi del muraglione del ponte,
tra i *drop out* della Roma città aperta,
apristi il tuo cuore all'insulto gratuito di Pedro,
tuo amante, e, basculandoti, cadesti nel vuoto,
disegnando traiettorie gravitazionali dal cielo al cemento.

Pedro, non eri ubriaco, ad un giorno di distanza,
non eri ubriaco, stato d'animo anormale,
nelle baraccopoli lungo l'alveo del Tevere,
o nelle serate vuote della movida milanese,
essendo intento a spiegare a cani e barboni
una curiosa lezione di geometria non euclidea.
Salito sui bordi del muraglione del ponte,
nell'indifferenza abulica dei tuoi scolari distratti,
saltasti, in cerca della stessa traiettoria d'amore,
dello stesso tragitto fatale alla tua Peggy,
atterrando, sul cemento, nello stesso istante.

I *punkabbestia* di Ponte Garibaldi, sgomberati dall'autorità
locale,

diffonderanno in ogni baraccopoli del mondo la lezione
surreale
imperniata sulla sbalorditiva idea
che l'amore sia un affare di geometria non euclidea.

The Ballad Of Peggy And Pedro

The ballad of Peggy and Pedro barked out by the
punkbestials
of the Garibaldi Bridge, with a mixture of hatred and
despair,
teaches us the intimate relationship between geometry and
love,
to love as if we were maths surrounded by stray dogs.

Peggy you were drunk, normal mood,
in the slums along the bed of the Tiber
and alcohol, on August evenings, doesn't warm you up,
clouding every sense in annihilating dreams,
transforming every chewed-up sentence into a gunfight in
the back
on armour dissolved by the summer heat.
Lying on the edges of the bridge's ledges,
among the drop-outs of the *Rome open city*,
you opened your heart to the gratuitous insult of Pedro,
your lover, and toppled over, falling into the void,
drawing gravitational trajectories from the sky to the
cement.

Pedro wasn't drunk, a day's journey away,
you weren't drunk, abnormal state of mind,
in the slums along the bed of the Tiber,
or in the empty parties of Milan's movida,
with the intention of explaining to dogs and tramps
a curious lesson of non-Euclidean geometry.
Mounted on the edge of the bridge,
in the apathetic indifference of your distracted pupils,
you jumped, in the same trajectory of love,

along the same fatal path as your Peggy,
landing on the cement at the same instant.

The punkbestials of the Garibaldi Bridge, cleared by the
local authority,
will spread a surreal lesson to every slum in the world
centred on the astonishing idea
that love is a matter of non-Euclidean geometry.

Ballata Degli Inesistenti

Potrei tentare di narrarvi
al suono della mia tastiera
come Baasima morì di lebbra
senza mai raggiunger la frontiera,
o come l'armeno Méroujan
sotto uno sventolio di mezzelune
sentì svanire l'aria dai suoi occhi
buttati via in una fossa comune;
Charlee, che travasata a Brisbane
in cerca di un mondo migliore,
concluse il viaggio
dentro le fauci di un alligatore,
o Aurélio, chiamato Bruna
che dopo otto mesi d'ospedale
morì di *aidiesse* contratto
a battere su una tangenziale.

Nessuno si ricorderà di Yehoudith,
delle sue labbra rosse carminio,
finite a bere veleni tossici
in un campo di sterminio,
o di Eerikki, dalla barba rossa, che,
sconfitto dalla smania di navigare,
dorme, raschiato dalle orche,
sui fondi d'un qualche mare;
la testa di Sandrine, duchessa
di Borgogna, udì rumor di festa
cadendo dalla lama d'una ghigliottina
in una cesta,
e Daisuke, moderno samurai,
del motore d'un aereo contava i giri
trasumanando un gesto da kamikaze
in harakiri.

Potrei starvi a raccontare

nell'afa d'una notte d'estate
come Iris ed Anthia, bimbe spartane
dacché deformi furono abbandonate,
o come Deendayal schiattò di stenti
imputabile dell'unico reato
di vivere una vita da intoccabile
senza mai essersi ribellato;
Ituha, ragazza indiana,
che, minacciata da un coltello,
finì a danzare con Manitou
nelle anticamere di un bordello,
e Luther, nato nel Lancashire,
che, liberato dal mestiere d'accattone,
fu messo a morire da sua maestà britannica
nelle miniere di carbone.

Chi si ricorderà di Itzayana,
e della sua famiglia massacrata
in un villaggio ai margini del Messico
dall'esercito di Carranza in ritirata,
e chi di Idris, africano ribelle,
tramortito dallo shock e dalle ustioni
mentre, indomito al dominio coloniale,
cercava di rubare un camion di munizioni;
Shahdi, volò alta nel cielo
sulle aste della verde rivoluzione,
atterrando a Teheran, le ali dilaniate
da un colpo di cannone,
e Tikhomir, muratore ceceno,
che rovinò tra i volti indifferenti
a terra dal tetto del Mausoleo
di Lenin, senza commenti.

Questi miei oggetti di racconto
fratti a frammenti di inesistenza
trasmettano suoni distanti
di resistenza.

Ballad Of The Non-Existent

I could try to tell you
with the sound of my keyboard
how Baasima died of leprosy
without ever reaching the border,
or how the Armenian Meroujan
under a flutter of half-moons
felt the air in his eyes vanish
thrown into a mass grave;
Charlee, who moved to Brisbane
in search of a better world,
ends the journey
in the mouth of an alligator,
or Aurelio, named Bruna
who, after eight months in hospital
died of AIDS contracted
to hit a ring road.

Nobody will remember Yehoudith,
her lips carmine red,
erased by drinking toxic poisons
in an extermination camp,
or Eerikki, with his red beard,
defeated by the turbulence of the waves,
who sleeps, scoured by orcas,
on the bottom of some sea;
the head of Sandrine, Duchess
of Burgundy heard the rumour of the feast
as it fell from the blade of a guillotine
into a basket
and Daisuke, modern samurai,
counted the revolutions of a plane's engine
transhumanizing a kamikaze gesture into harakiri.

I could go on and on
in the stifling heat of a summer night

how Iris and Anthia, deformed Spartan children
were abandoned,
or how Deendayal died of deprivation
attributable to the single crime
of living the life of an outcast
without ever having rebelled;
Ituha, an Indian girl,
threatened with a knife,
who ends up dancing with Manitou
in the anteroom of a brothel
and Luther, born in Lancashire
freed from the profession of beggar
and forced to die by His Britannic Majesty
in the coal mines.

Who will remember Itzayana
and her family massacred
in a village on the outskirts of Mexico
by Carranza's retreating army,
and what of Idris, the African rebel,
stunned by shocks and burns
while untamed by colonial domination,
he tried to steal an ammunition truck;
Shahdi flew high into the sky
above the flagpoles of the Green Revolution,
landing in Tehran with his wings torn apart
by a cannon shot,
and Tikhomir, a Chechen bricklayer,
that fell among the indifferent faces
to the ground from the roof of Lenin's Mausoleum,
without comment.

From objects of narrative
fractured into fragments of non-existence
transmits distant sounds
of resistance.

Ivan Pozzoni

Ram Krishna Singh

Aram Krishna Singh

Ram Krishna Singh has been writing for over four decades now . Born (31 December 1950), brought up and educated in Varanasi, he has been professionally concerned with ELT and IWE. A retired Professor at IIT-ISM in Dhanbad, Dr Singh has published 25 poetry collections, including *Silencio: Blanca desconfianza: Silence: White distrust* (Spanish/English, 2021), *A Lone Sparrow* (e-book English/Arabic, 2021), *Against the Waves: Selected Poems* (2021), 白濁: *SILENCE: A WHITE DISTRUST* (English/Japanese, 2022), *Poems and Micropoems* (2023), and *Knocking Vistas And Other Poems* (2024). Find him on X (Twitter) *@profrksingh* and on Facebook www.facebook.com/profrksingh .

More at: https://pennyspoetry.wikia.com/wiki/R.K._Singh .
email: profrksingh@gmail.com

Freaky Bodies

Mood of the moment
seductive in dullness
eternal eros:
changing constantly inside
now says she hates my scent

taunting the old pain
in the brothel of bed
kitchen or shower
she fears the freaky bodies
snaky arousal and peak

through sucking hisses
thuds and soft screams repeated
in sync dripping down
until next round of silence
with back to each other

Abrupt Notes

Intentionally layered
internally fragmented
queer antics:

she builds up her own
sexual toolkit to prove
how coward man is

she sees a rapist
in each man detests
the male smell but trusts
one night stand
with deep thrust
long erections
and climax control
for blood to soak smoothly

she sits shrouded
in her see-through pink gown
on the terrace
inviting autumn winds
for longer stopover
just to accuse the artist
of invading her body

she curses a young bull
for obstructing her way
in the street shouts at hawkers

and, yet another
at eighty re-imagines
fading memories
with snaky radiance
to break a new dawn

Aram Krishna Singh

my friend says
the dynamics change:
there's a before
and an after
to feel life

I say yes, but I'm tired
of walking and writing
what I watch

I'm no tout to comfort
or restore the faith
of a dwindling flock in heat
culling is convenient

Tanka:

she gives him the push
when he says sex starving
is a greater sin
than fasting for his long life
or praying to the *lingam*

***

after a tiff
lying under the same blanket
two of us stare
the peeping moon and turn
with glee to each other

***

shaped like a bird
a drop of water lands
on her breast:
my breath jumps to kiss it
before her pelvic flick

***

weaving no web
a dark fishing spider
mates in the creek
and curls up hanging from the twat
in one-shot deal

***

Stains of honeymoon
the sun and clouds:
sky's gentle embrace

Aram Krishna Singh

time can't erase
hues of passion

***

I clasp your hands
and feel the blood
running savagely
through your arteries
in tulip silence

***

her beauty
smells the soil that sings
grace in look:
I whisper my heart and chase
the glow her shadow spreads

***

the wind lifts
her curved nudity
in the water curtain
I touch the strings that whisper
love in each falling drop

***

unquenched thirst
more and more indulgence:
momentary pleasure
she says it's enough now
rein the horse and seek the missed

Ibrahim

Honjo

Ibrahim Honjo

Ibrahim Honjo is a Canadian/Bosnian poet-writer, who writes in Bosnian, and English language. He has worked as an economist, journalist, editor, marketing director, and property manager. He is currently retired and resides in Canada.

Honjo is author 26 published books in Bosnian Language, (8 books in English, 3 books bilingually (in English and Bosnian language). In addition, 5 joints' books of poems published with Serbian poets. His poems have been represented in more than 90 world anthologies, and more than 60 literary magazines.

Some of Honjo's poems have been translated into Italian, Spanish, Korean, Polish, Slovenian, Bahasa (Malaysia), Mongolian, Turkmen, Turkish, Russian, Bengali, Portuguese, French, Thai, Arabic, Tajik, Vietnamese, Chinese, Macedonian, Filipino, Persian and German.
He received several prizes for his poetry.

What About Tomorrow

Today I am the one conflicting in me
I from the past
I from the present
I from the future
Wars are springing like mushrooms
Necks are broken
I from the past, am bleeding
I from the present, am bleeding
I from the future, am bleeding
In me today
Today in me
Cannons are roaring
Like the insides of a mountain
While earthquakes are going on
Sites of fire are burning after battles
And in me
I from the past
I from the present
I from the future
And nothing else
Winners leave and pass by with laurels
I with a curse

Who will bury me tomorrow?

The Stone

They never asked me
For my name
They wanted my identity card
Or its number

I did not have one

I said Stone

They laughed
Asked me where I was from

From the stone - I said

They asked for my age

Twenty pebbles – I answered
And showed them gray spotted pebbles

They are opening their hearts to me
I am closing the doorway on the invisible wall
Which divides us
I am going away

Disharmony

Blue
Blue
I am passing, crawling
By the azure sleeplessness
I harmonize hunger with winter disharmony
With ghosts and sycophants
Slander blue snows
I fall asleep in bear's pool of mud
In the morning, I wake up with thorns in sight
I take bears as blood brothers
In some powerful blueness
And then using a stick made of a black thorn
I count the news
And line up illusions
Until the day comes
While from everything
Only disharmony is left

Kazimierz Burnat

Kazimierz Burnat

Kazimierz Burnat, Polish poet, essayist, translator of Slavic literature, journalist, literary critic, culture animator... Author of 23 poetry books (7 translations from Czech and Ukrainian) and more than 60 collective books in translation. Co-author of approx. 370 anthologies and monographs. Rendered into at least 44 languages. Organizer of the International Poetry Festival "Poets Without Borders" in Polanica-Zdrój. Honored with Silver Medal "For Merit to Culture Gloria Artis", Minister of Culture and National Heritage Award (2023), Shabdaguchha International Poetry Award (USA / Bangladesh 2023), among others. From 2015, President of the Lower Silesian Branch of the Polish Writers' Union.

Retreat

I am afraid of lost time
it intensifies the malaise
of an escape into creativity
and one needs to immerse oneself in it
compulsively desperately
to enslave fear
out of books building a barricade
against the massacred truth
against hatred

writing – a nightmare
I have become a poet
requiring correction
and changes
pinch the authenticity

I must necessarily
engraft wild words
overheard in dreams
to anew be able to
express myself and the world
in the best possible way

Translated by Anna Maria Stępień

Not death separates people
but lack of love.
Jim Morrison

Love
is wild flowers
simplicity-colored

the sky's clear azure

soul and flesh entwined
by a flimsy unity

it is you and him
in the glow of trust
showing the common path
to Sesame

love
is an ebony tunnel
with bedazzlement at the end

not seeing
will arouse new sensations

Translated by Anna Maria Stępień

Wrongheadedness

Discouraged by waiting
for prosperity
they abandon the pretense of bonds

though unripe are the common fruit
ready to pollinate
wayside flowers
already burdened with a flaw

distrust
makes them the carriers of hatred
indwelling the innermost resources

and so
nestled into foreign tenderness
hearing the pulse bubbling
of leaky hearts
they savor the image of unfulfillment

from breathlessness
souls grow blue

the final wake-up call
for a compromise lesson

Translated by Anna Maria Stępień

Remembering

our fallen soldiers of verse

Janet Perkins Caldwell

February 14, 1959 ~ September 20, 2016

Alan W. Jankowski

16 March 1961 ~ 10 March 2017

Shareef Abdur Rasheed

30 May 1945 ~ 11 February 2025

The Butterfly Effect

"IS" in effect

Inner Child Press

News

Published Books

by

Poetry Posse Members

We are so excited to share and announce a few of the current books, as well as the new and upcoming books of some of our Poetry Posse authors.

On the following pages we present to you ...

Alicja Maria Kuberska

Jackie Davis Allen

Gail Weston Shazor

hülya n. yılmaz

Nizar Sartawi

Elizabeth E. Castillo

Faleeha Hassan

Fahredin Shehu

Kimberly Burnham

Caroline 'Ceri' Nazareno

Eliza Segiet

Teresa E. Gallion

Mutawaf Shaheed

William S. Peters, Sr.

Now Available

www.innerchildpress.com

KREW ŻYCIA

The Blood of Life

Eliza Segiet

Translated by Dorota Stępińska

Now Available
www.innerchildpress.com

An Ode to Love

Love Prevails

William S. Peters, Sr.

Now Available

Now Available

I Am in Your Head

C. E. Shy

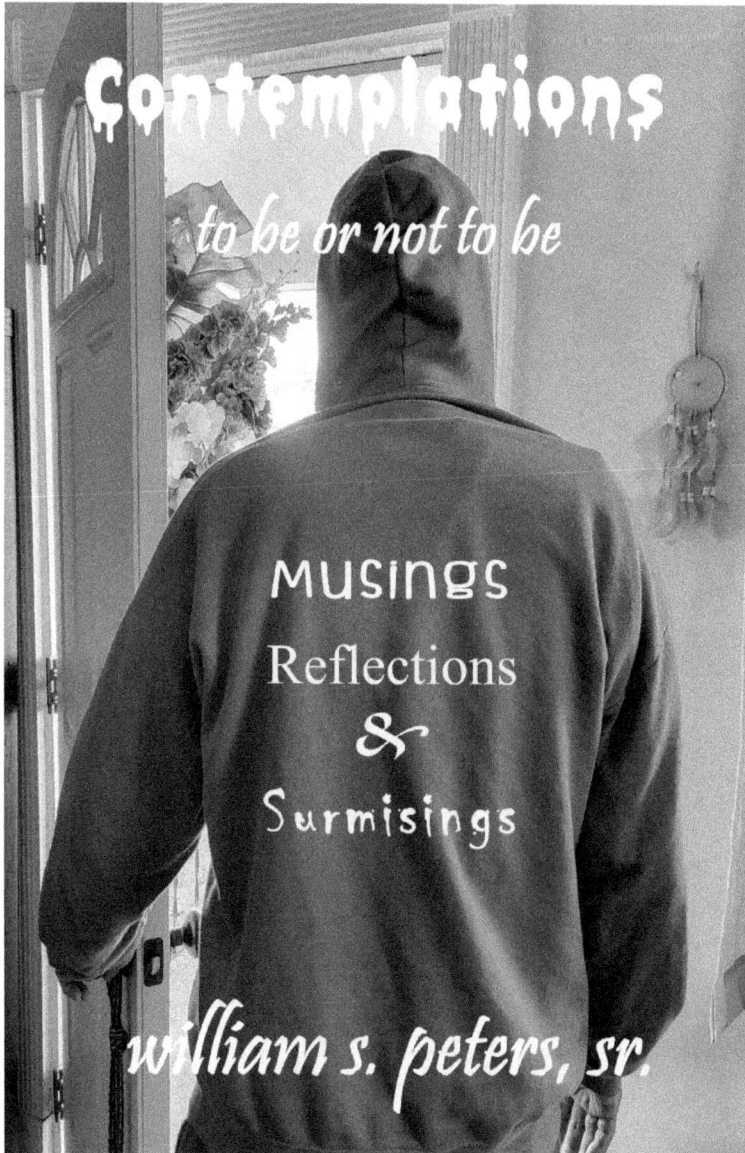

Contemplations

to be or not to be

musings

Reflections

&

Surmisings

william s. peters, sr.

Inner Child Press News

Now Available

www.innerchildpress.com

Come Egypt

Poetry by

Teresa E. Gallion

Now Available

www.innerchildpress.com

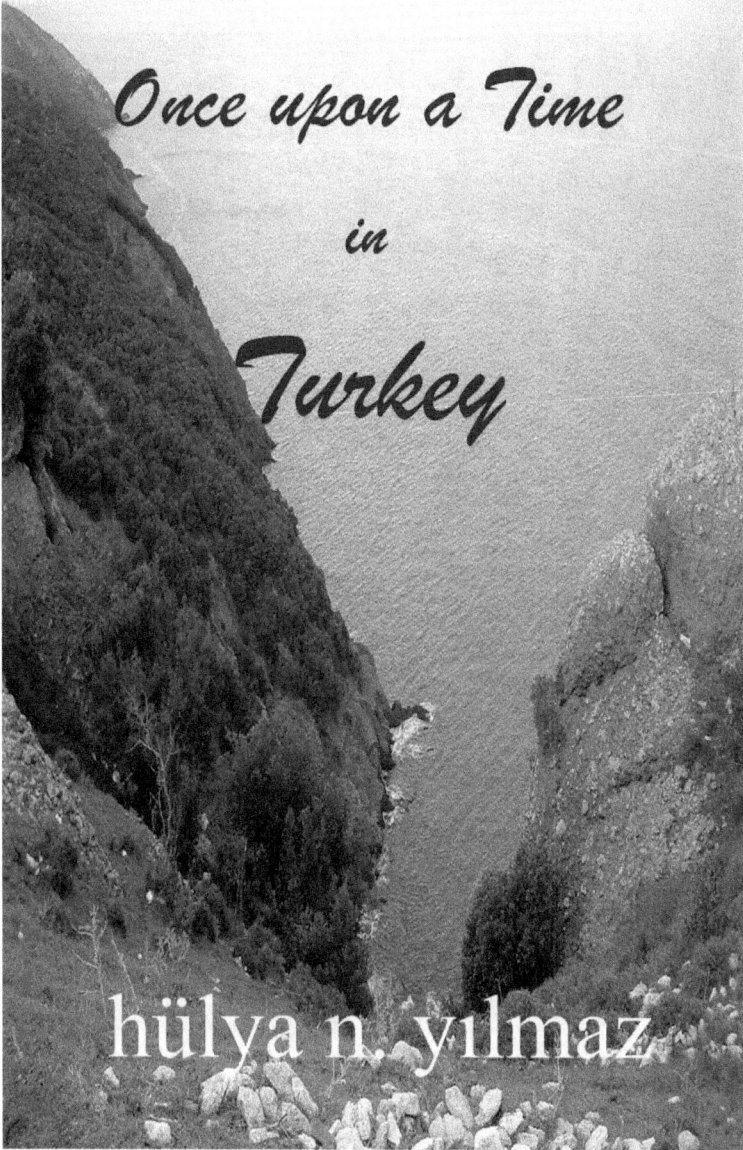

Once upon a Time

in

Turkey

hülya n. yılmaz

Now Available
www.innerchildpress.com

Unapologetically

BLACK

&

Blues

william s. peters, sr.

Now Available
www.innerchildpress.com

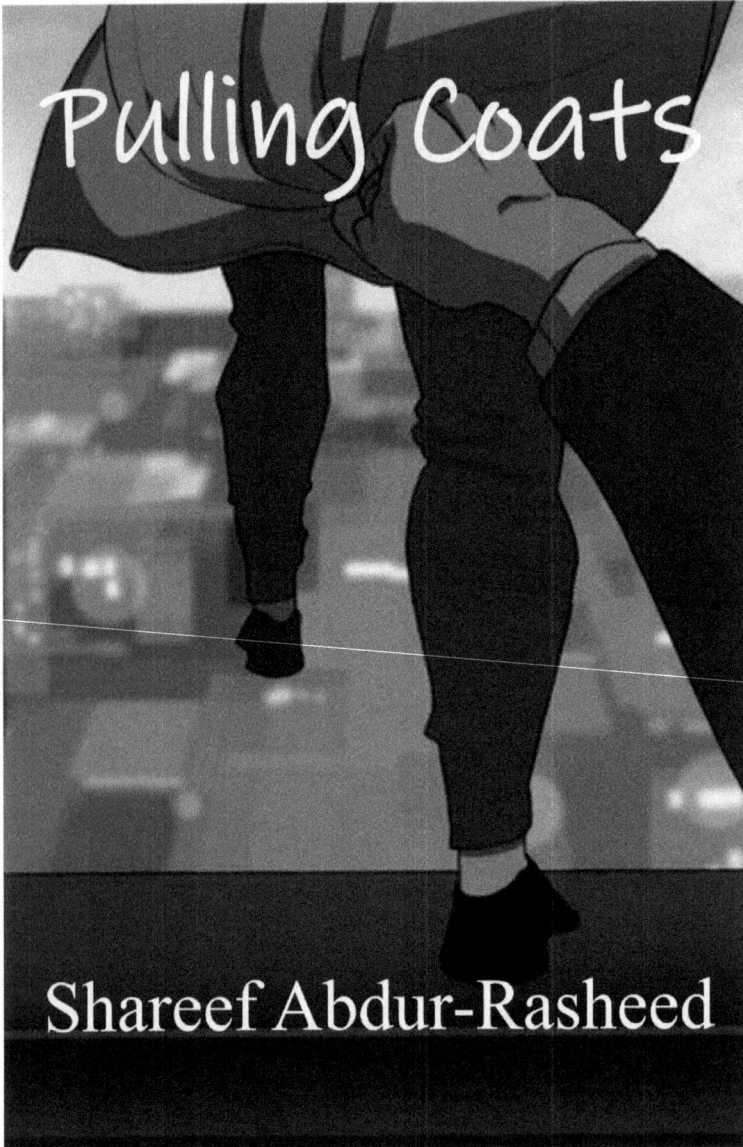

Pulling Coats

Shareef Abdur-Rasheed

Now Available
www.innerchildpress.com

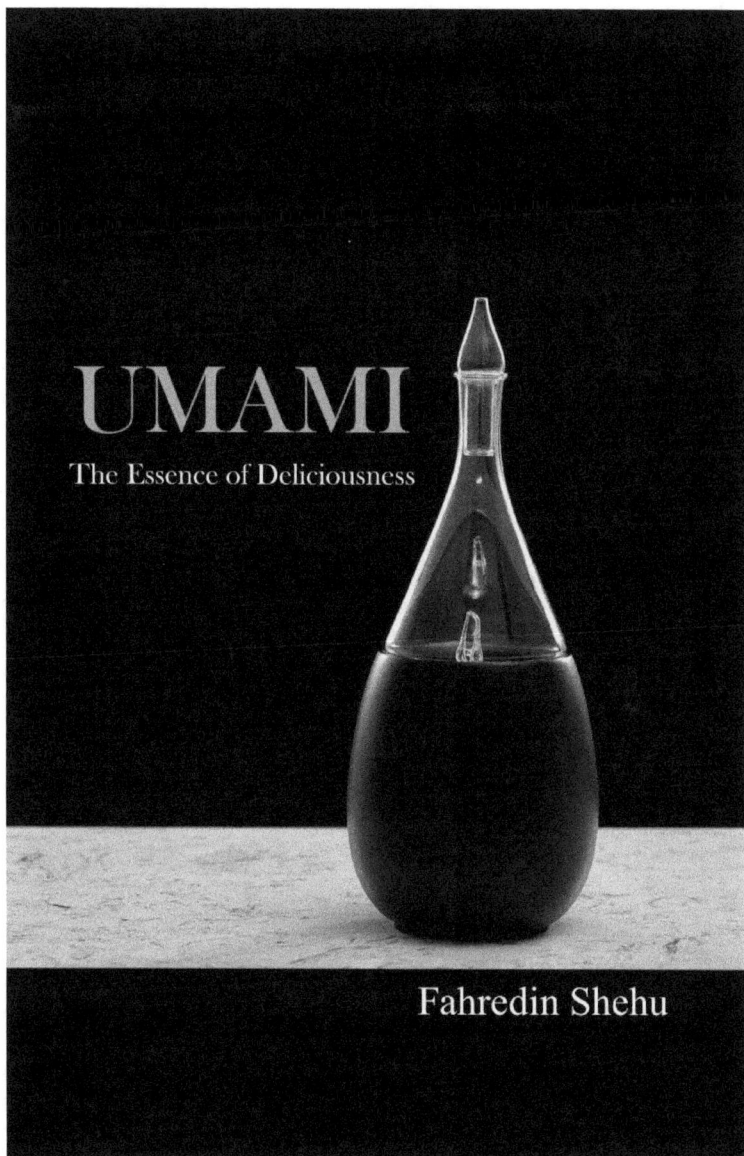

UMAMI

The Essence of Deliciousness

Fahredin Shehu

Now Available

www.innerchildpress.com

After the Frost

Alicja Maria Kuberska

Now Available
www.innerchildpress.com

Fahredin Shehu

ORMUS

Now Available
www.innerchildpress.com

Ahead of My Time

. . . from the Streets to the Stages

Albert 'Infinite' Carrasco

Now Available

www.innerchildpress.com

Eliza Segiet

To Be More

Now Available at
www.innerchildpress.com

SEARCH FOR THE MAGICAL
MULTILINGUAL FROG

A Tale of Ribbit in 50 Languages

KIMBERLY BURNHAM

Now Available at

www.amazon.com/gp/product/B08MYL5B7S/ref=
dbs_a_def_rwt_hsch_vapi_tkin_p1_i2

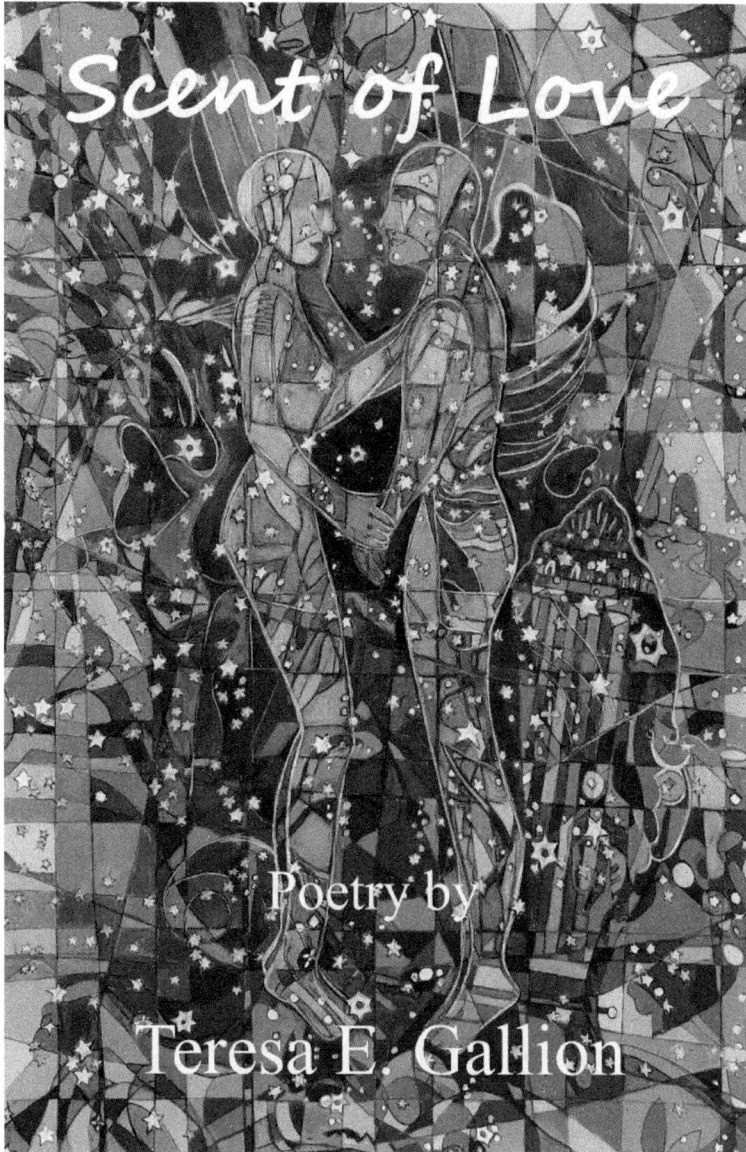

Scent of Love

Poetry by

Teresa E. Gallion

Now Available
www.innerchildpress.com

Inner Reflections

of the
Muse

Elizabeth Castillo

Now Available
www.innerchildpress.com

Letter - Poems

from a Beloved

hülya n. yılmaz

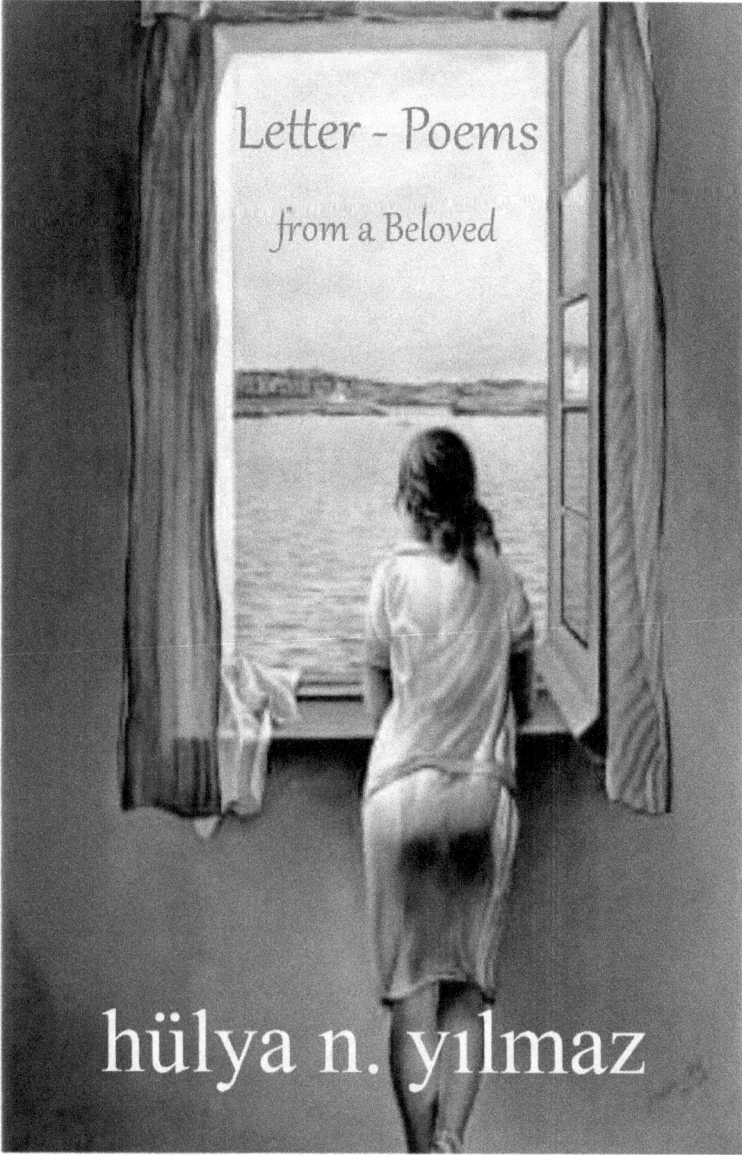

Now Available
www.innerchildpress.com

The
Utah
Chronicles

William S. Peters, Sr.

Now Available
www.innerchildpress.com

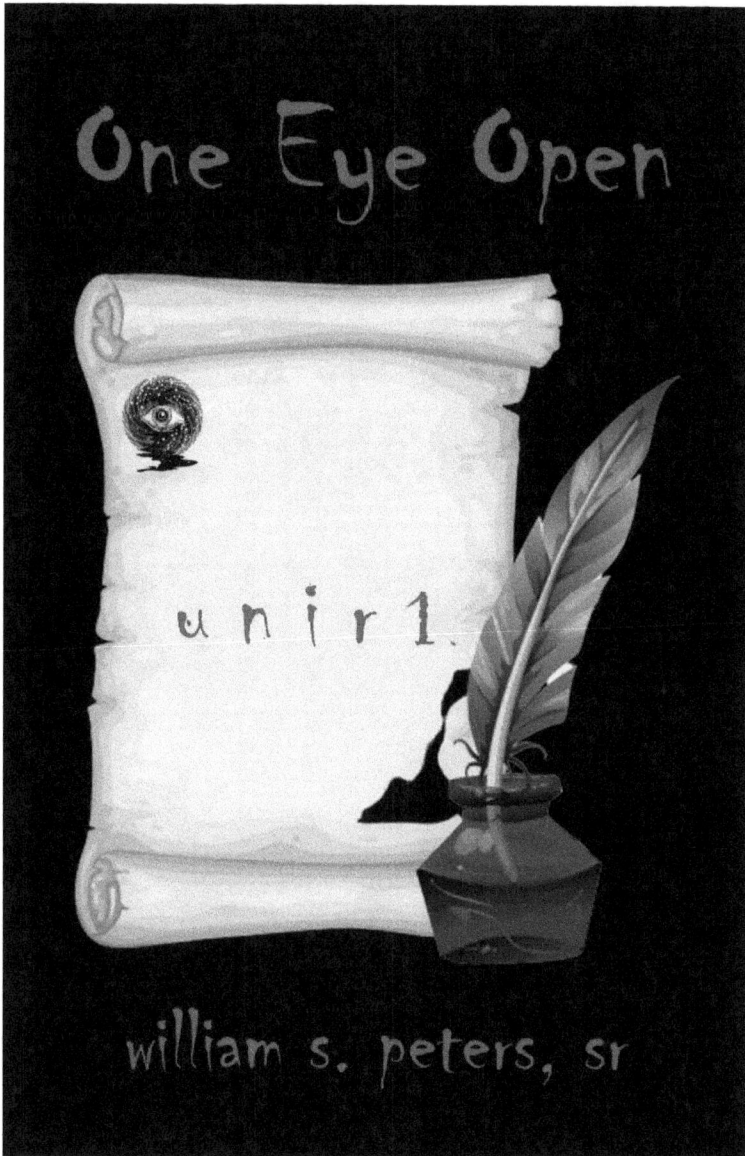

One Eye Open

u n i r 1.

william s. peters, sr

Now Available

www.innerchildpress.com

The Book of krisar

volume v

william s. peters, sr.

Now Available

www.innerchildpress.com

The Book of krisar

Volume I

william s. peters, sr.

The Book of krisar

Volume II

william s. peters, sr.

Now Available

www.innerchildpress.com

The Book of krisar

Volume III

william s. peters, sr.

The Book of krisar

Volume IV

william s. peters, sr.

Now Available

www.innerchildpress.com

Velvet Passions

of

Calibrated Quarks

Caroline Nazareno-Gabis

Now Available
www.innerchildpress.com

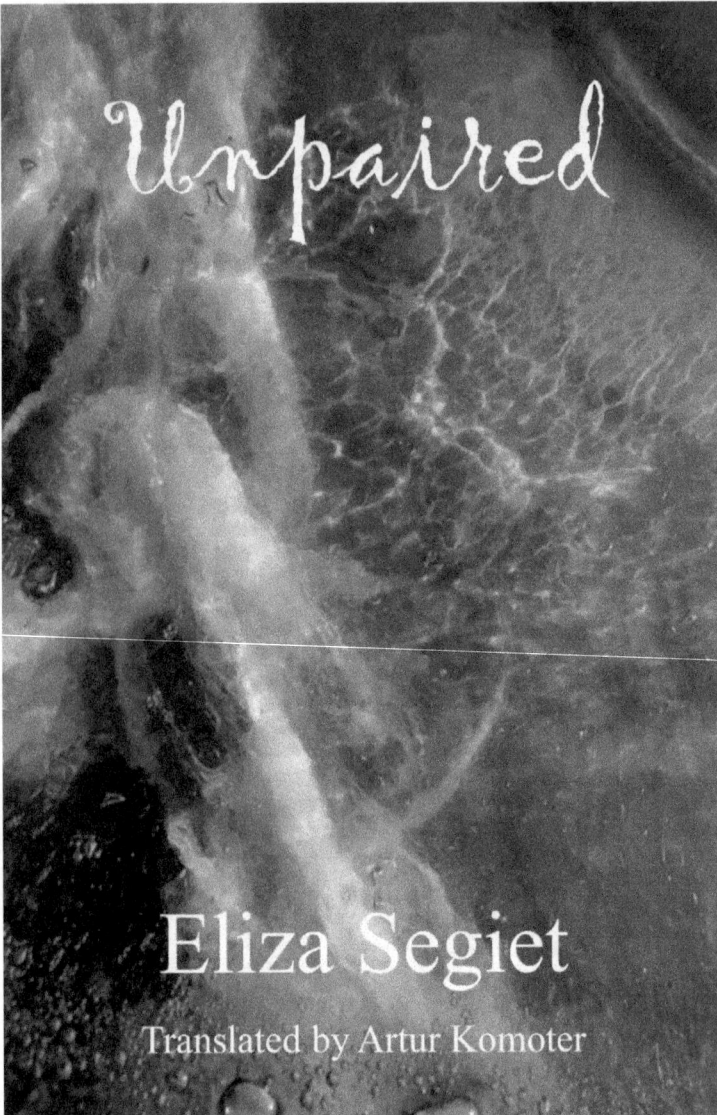

Unpaired

Eliza Segiet

Translated by Artur Komoter

Now Available

www.innerchildpress.com

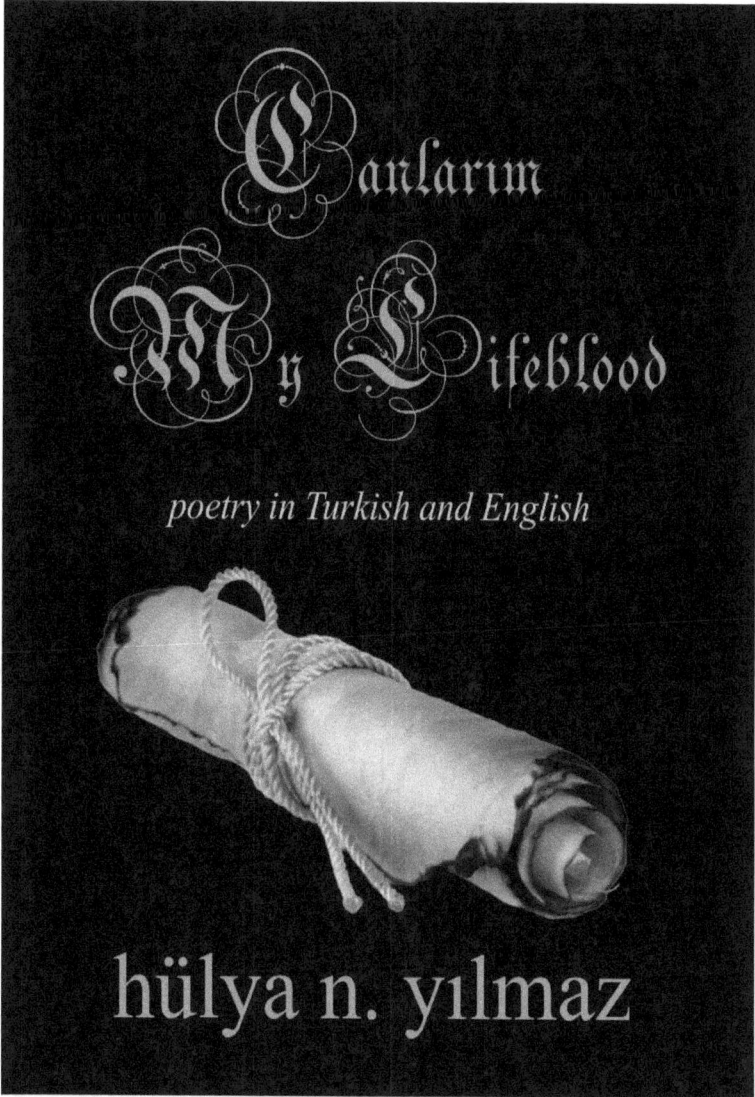

Canlarım

My Lifeblood

poetry in Turkish and English

hülya n. yılmaz

Private Issue
www.innerchildpress.com

Butterfly's Voice

Faleeha Hassan

Translated by William M. Hutchins

Now Available at
www.innerchildpress.com

No Illusions

Through the Looking Glass

Jackie Davis Allen

Now Available at
www.innerchildpress.com

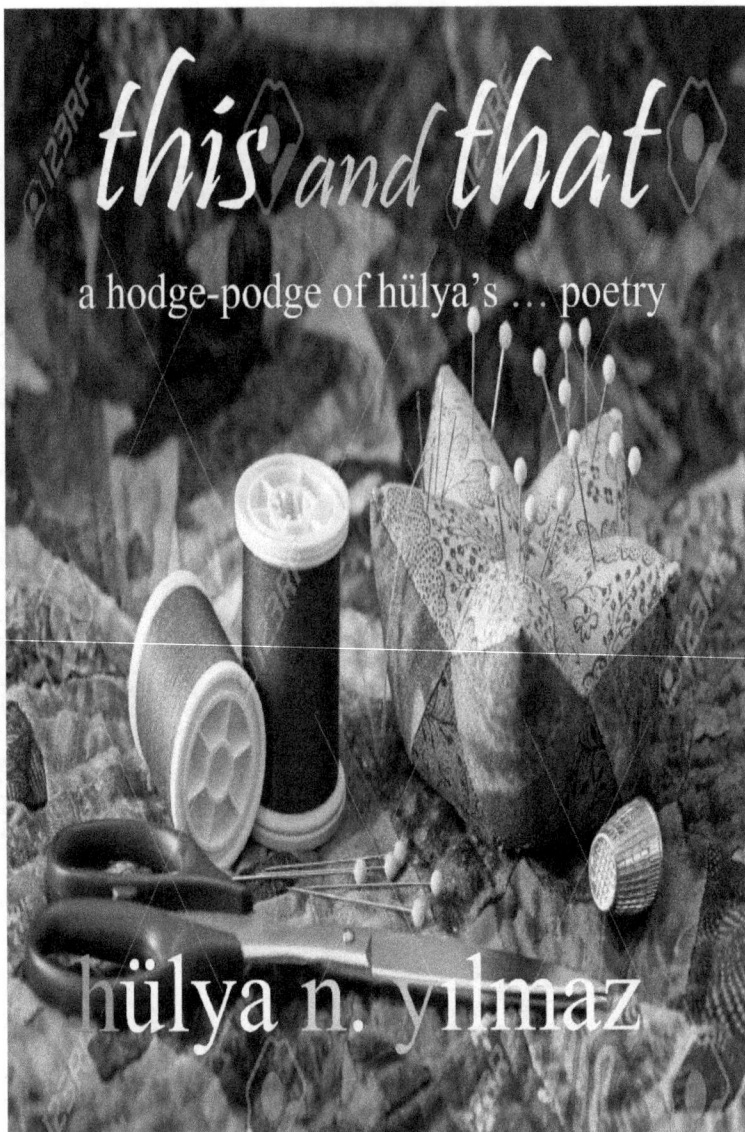

this and that

a hodge-podge of hülya's ... poetry

hülya n. yılmaz

Now Available at
www.innerchildpress.com

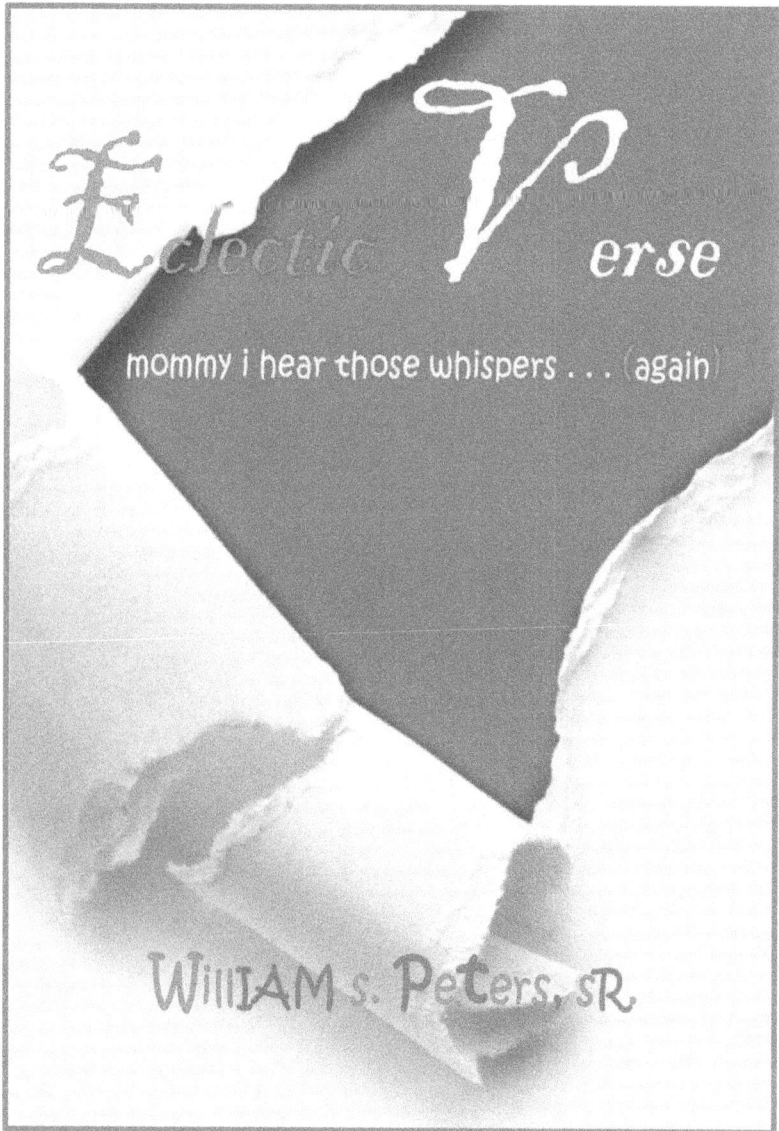

Now Available at
www.innerchildpress.com

HERENOW

◆

FAHREDIN SHEHU

Now Available at
www.innerchildpress.com

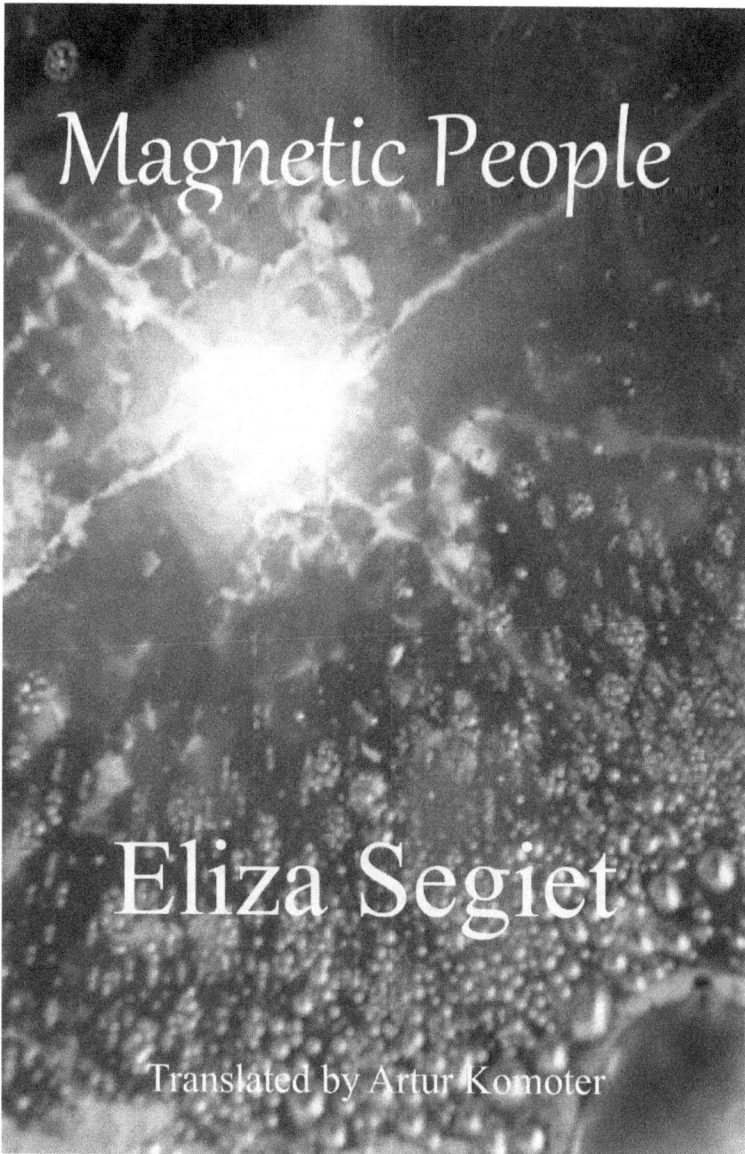

Magnetic People

Eliza Segiet

Translated by Artur Komoter

Now Available at
www.innerchildpress.com

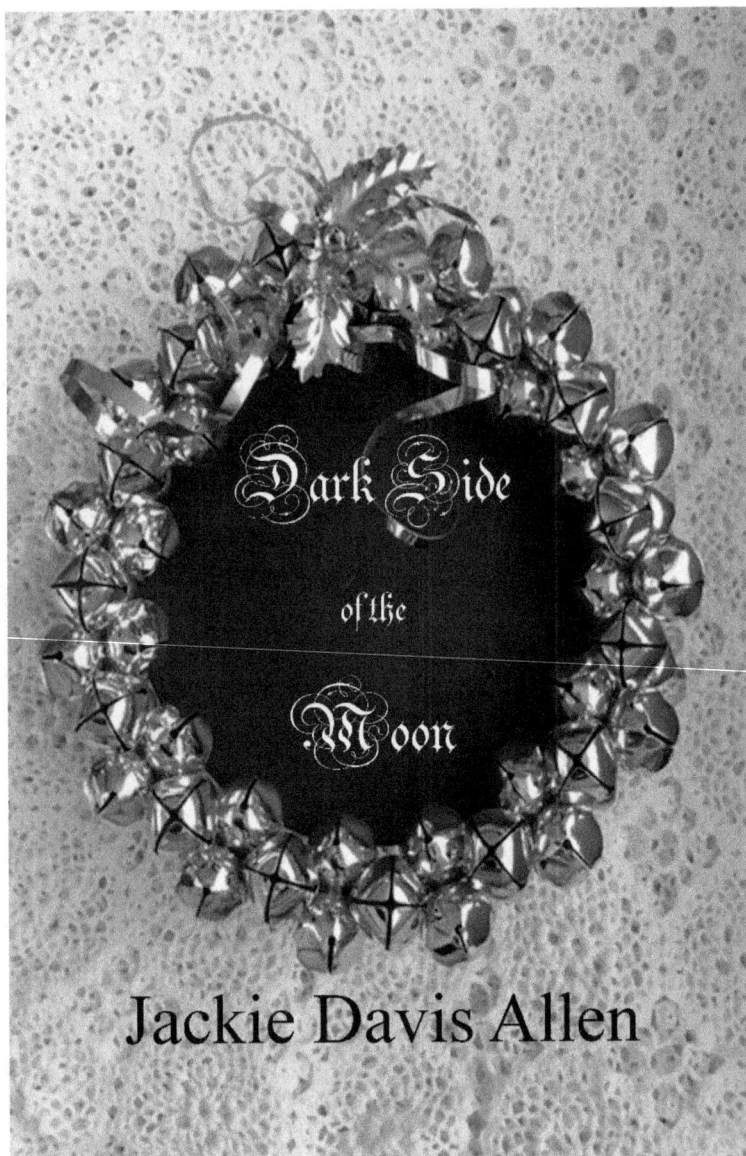

Dark Side
of the
Moon

Jackie Davis Allen

Now Available at
www.innerchildpress.com

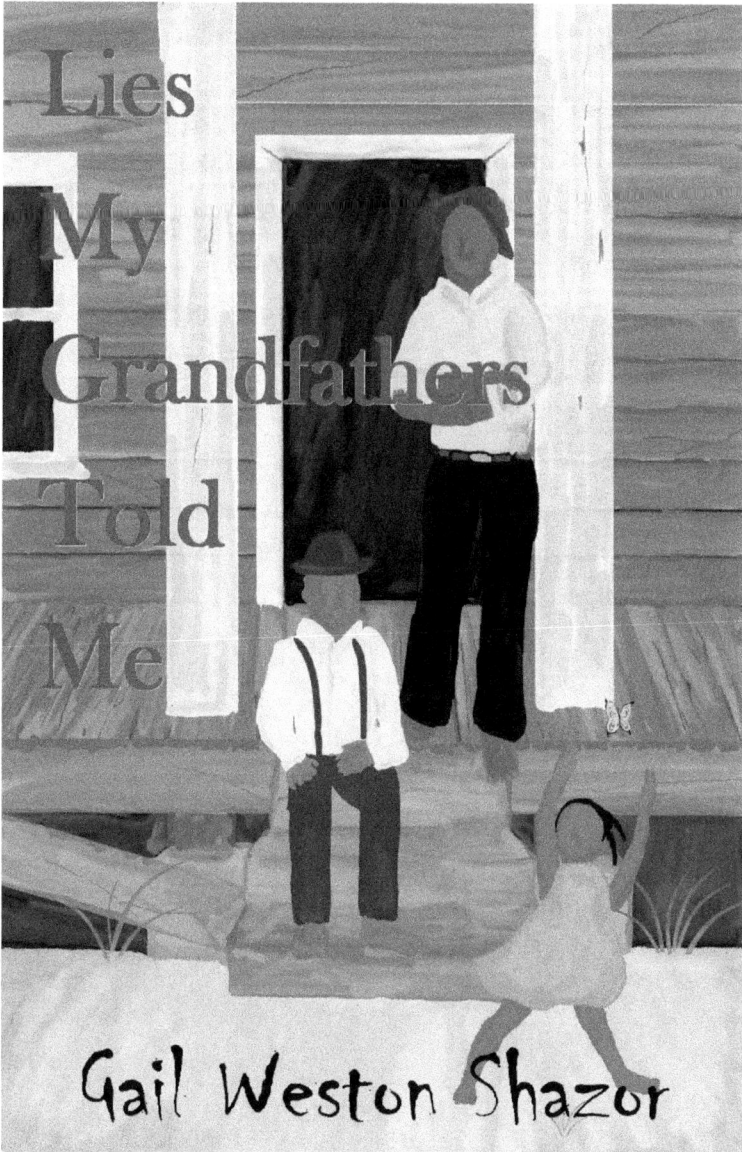

Lies
My
Grandfathers
Told
Me

Gail Weston Shazor

Now Available at
www.innerchildpress.com

Aflame

Memoirs in Verse

hülya n. yılmaz

Now Available at
www.innerchildpress.com

Mass Graves

Faleeha Hassan

Now Available at
www.innerchildpress.com

Breakfast

for

Butterflies

Faleeha Hassan

Now Available at

www.innerchildpress.com

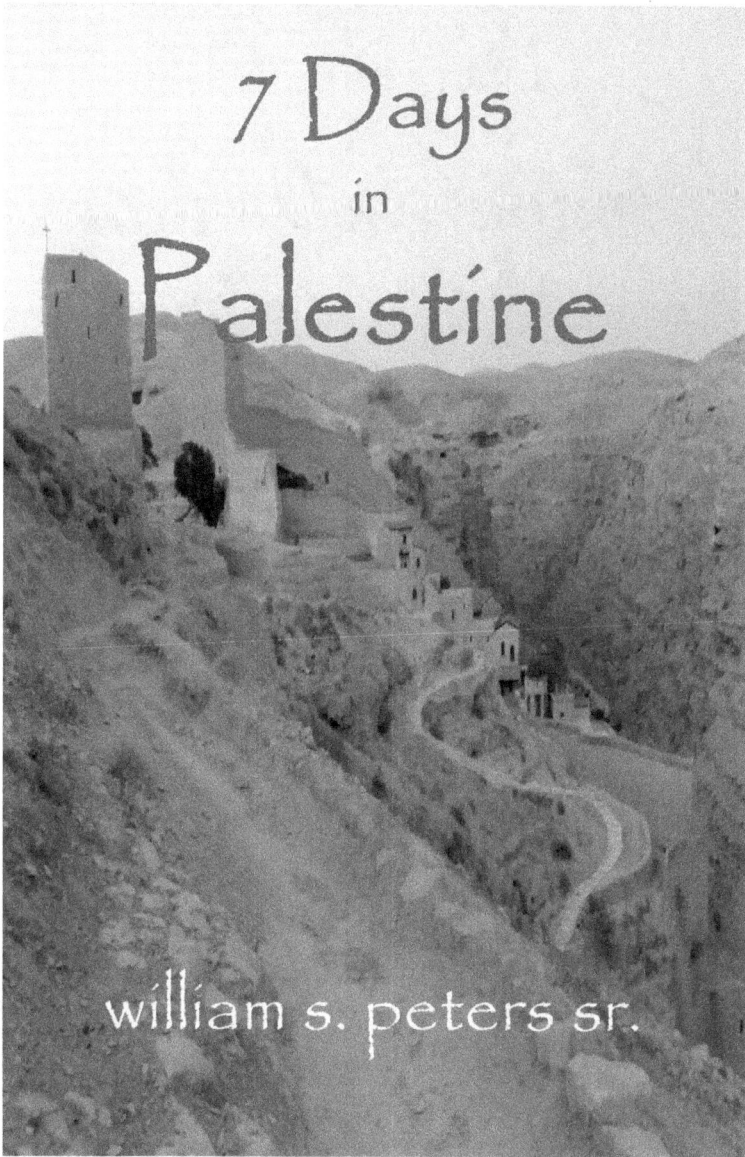

7 Days
in
Palestine

william s. peters sr.

Now Available at
www.innerchildpress.com

inner child press
presents

Tunisian Dreams

william s. peters, sr.

Now Available at
www.innerchildpress.com

INNER CHILD PRESS

THIS IS WHY I SLEEP

william s. peters sr.

Now Available at
www.innerchildpress.com

my inner garden

~ expressions and discoveries ~

by

William S. Peters, Sr.

Now Available

www.innerchildpress.com

Other
Anthological
works from

Inner Child Press International

www.innerchildpress.com

Shareef

a soldier for

Allah

Patriarch, Activist & Humanitarian

Friends of the Pen

Now Available

www.innerchildpress.com/anthologies

Inner Child Press International

presents

W.A.R"

We Are Revolution

Too Much Blood

Poets for Humanity

Now Available

www.innerchildpress.com

I want my poetry to... *volume* 4

the conscious poets

inspired by . . . Monte Smith

Now Available

www.innerchildpress.com/anthologies

Now Available

www.innerchildpress.com/anthologies

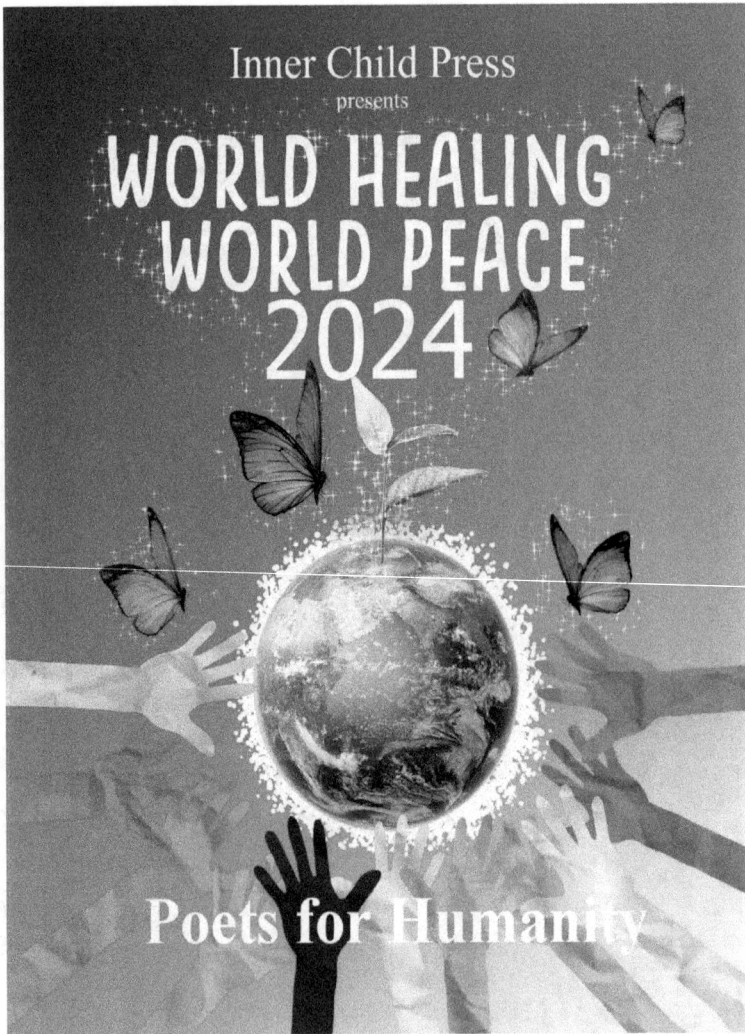

Inner Child Press

presents

WORLD HEALING WORLD PEACE 2024

Poets for Humanity

Now Available

www.worldhealingworldpeacepoetry.com

World Healing
World Peace
2022

Poets for Humanity

Now Available

www.innerchildpress.com/anthologies

World Healing World Peace
2020

Poets for Humanity

Now Available

www.worldhealingworldpeacepoetry.com

I want to
Live

an examination of Black & White issues

POETRY

ANALYSES

STORIES

creative
writing

critical essays

WRITERS FOR HUMANITY

Now Available

www.innerchildpress.com/anthologies

Inner Child Press International
&
The Year of the Poet
present

Poetry
the best of 2020

Poets of the World

Now Available

www.innerchildpress.com/anthologies

Inner Child Press International

presents

W.A.R.

We Are Revolution

Poets for Humanity

Now Available
www.innerchildpress.com/anthologies

the Heart of a Poet

words for a better tomorrow

The Conscious Poets

Now Available

www.innerchildpress.com/anthologies

Corona

Social Distancing

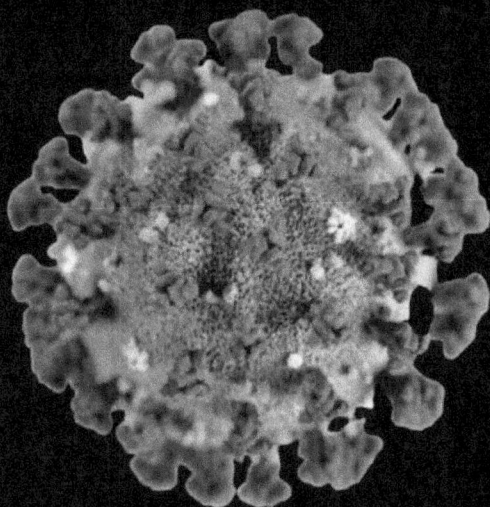

Poets for Humanity

Now Available

www.innerchildpress.com/anthologies

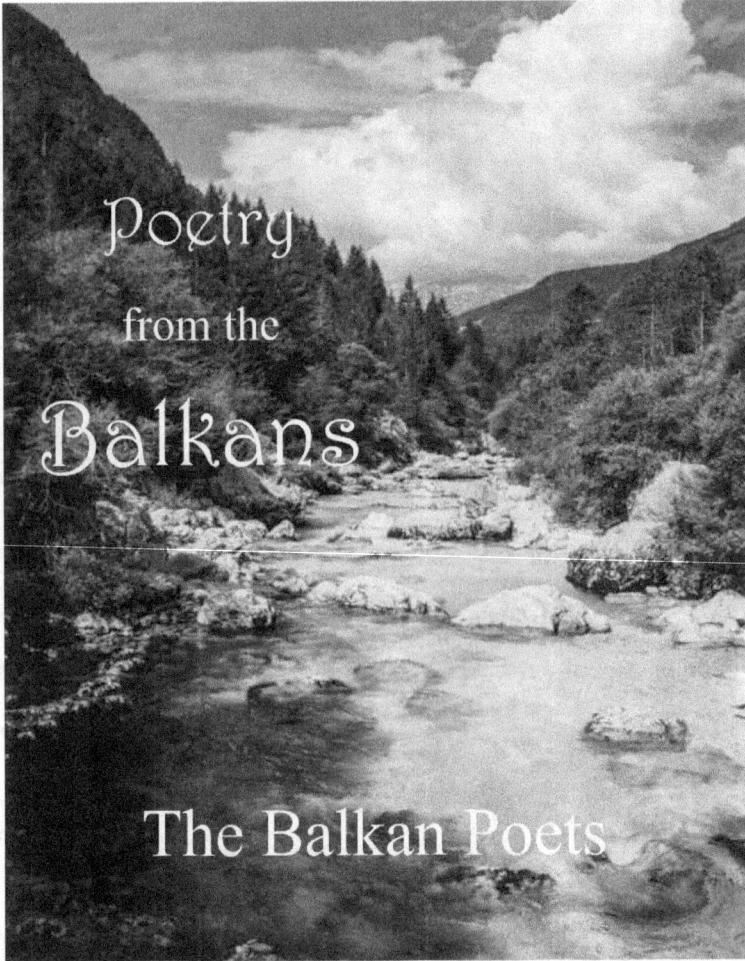

Poetry

from the

Balkans

The Balkan Poets

Now Available

www.innerchildpress.com/anthologies

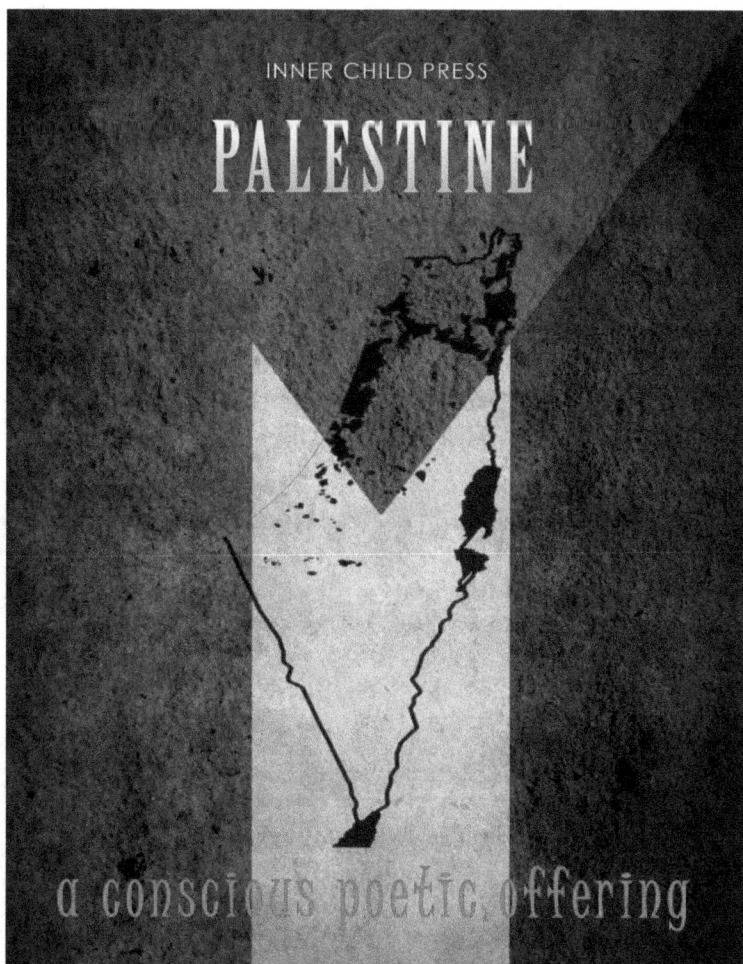

INNER CHILD PRESS

PALESTINE

a conscious poetic offering

Now Available

www.innerchildpress.com/anthologies

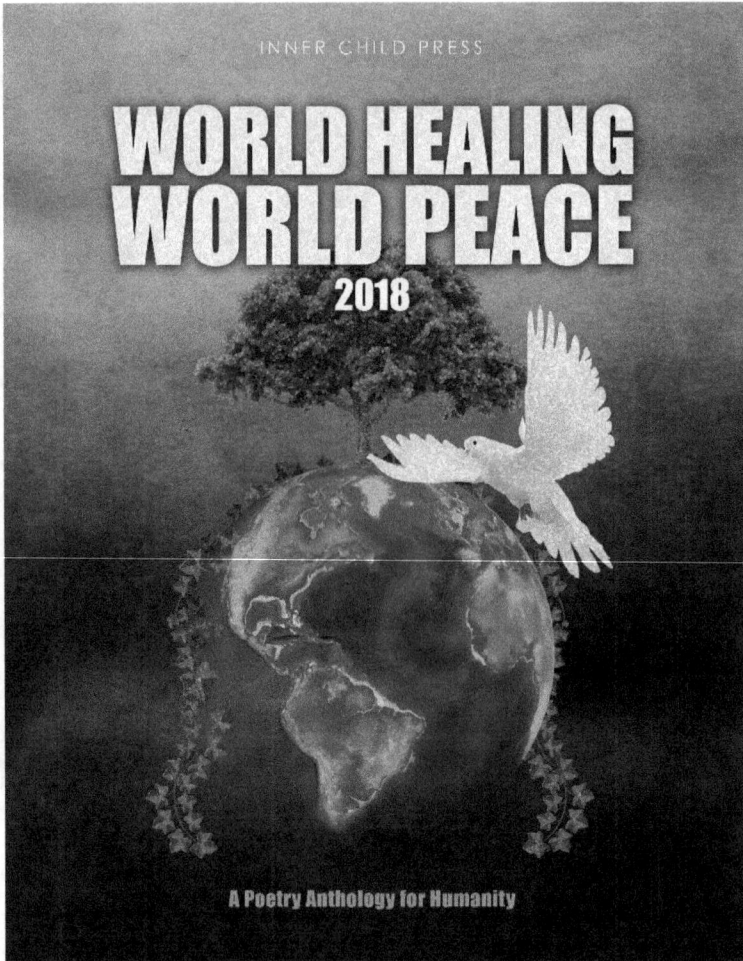

Now Available

www.innerchildpress.com/anthologies

Inner Child Press International
presents

𝔄 𝔏𝔬𝔳𝔢 𝔄𝔫𝔱𝔥𝔬𝔩𝔬𝔤𝔶

2019

The Love Poets

Now Available

www.innerchildpress.com/anthologies

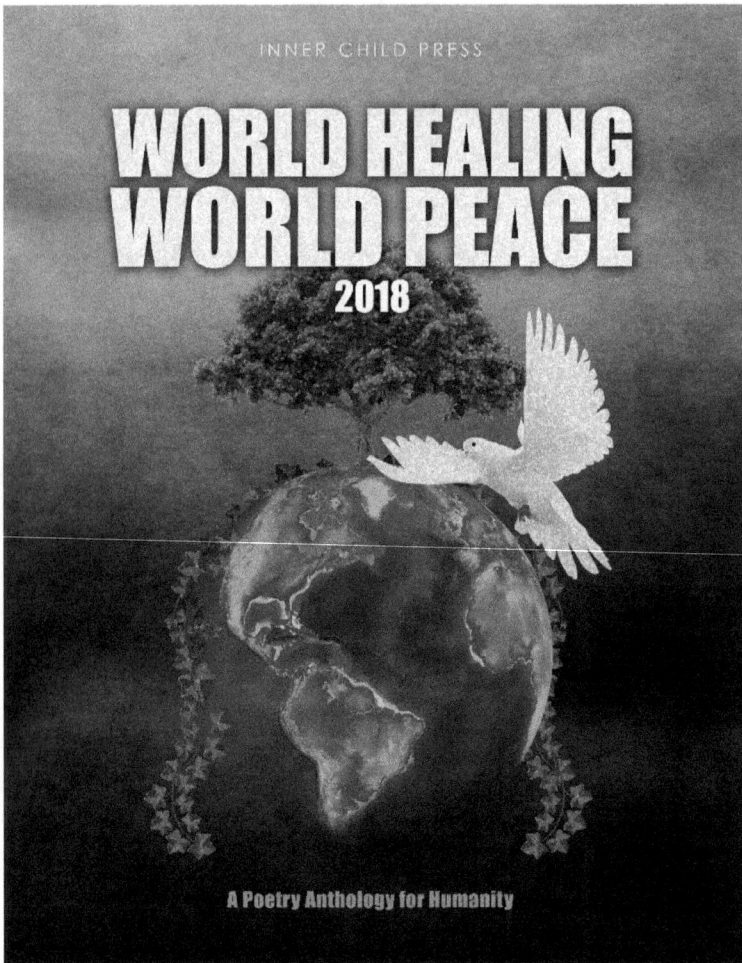

INNER CHILD PRESS

WORLD HEALING
WORLD PEACE
2018

A Poetry Anthology for Humanity

Now Available

www.worldhealingworldpeacepoetry.com

Now Available

www.worldhealingworldpeacepoetry.com

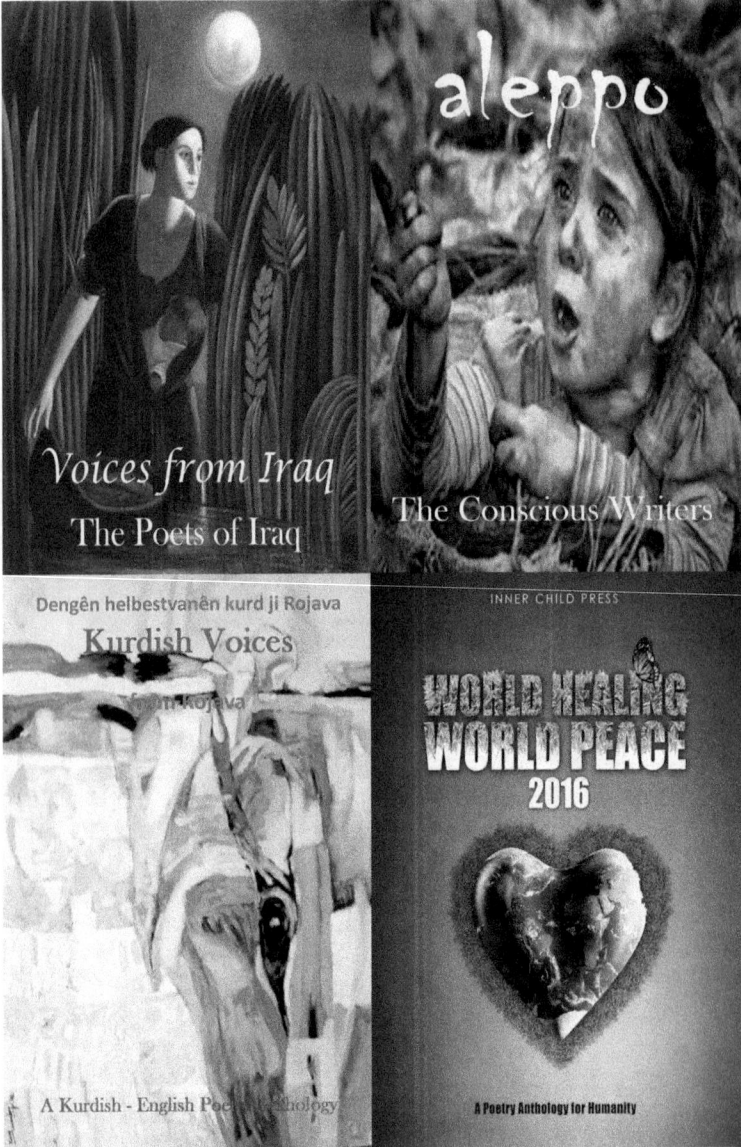

Now Available

www.innerchildpress.com/anthologies

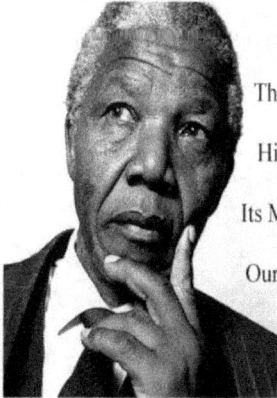

Mandela

The Man

His Life

Its Meaning

Our Words

Poetry . . . Commentary & Stories
The Anthological Writers

A GATHERING OF WORDS

POETRY & COMMENTARY
FOR
TRAYVON MARTIN

INNER CHILD PRESS

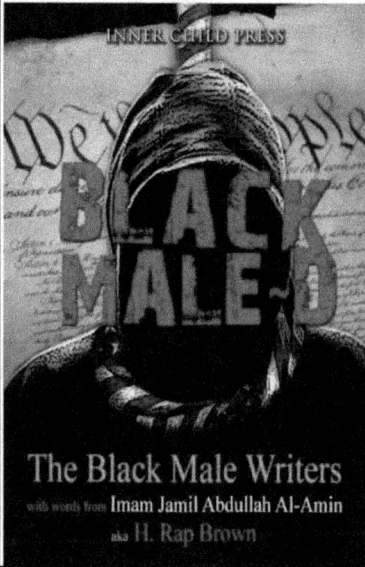

BLACK MALE-D

The Black Male Writers
with words from Imam Jamil Abdullah Al-Amin
aka H. Rap Brown

I

want

my

poetry

to... volume 4

the conscious poets

inspired by . . . Monte Smith

Now Available

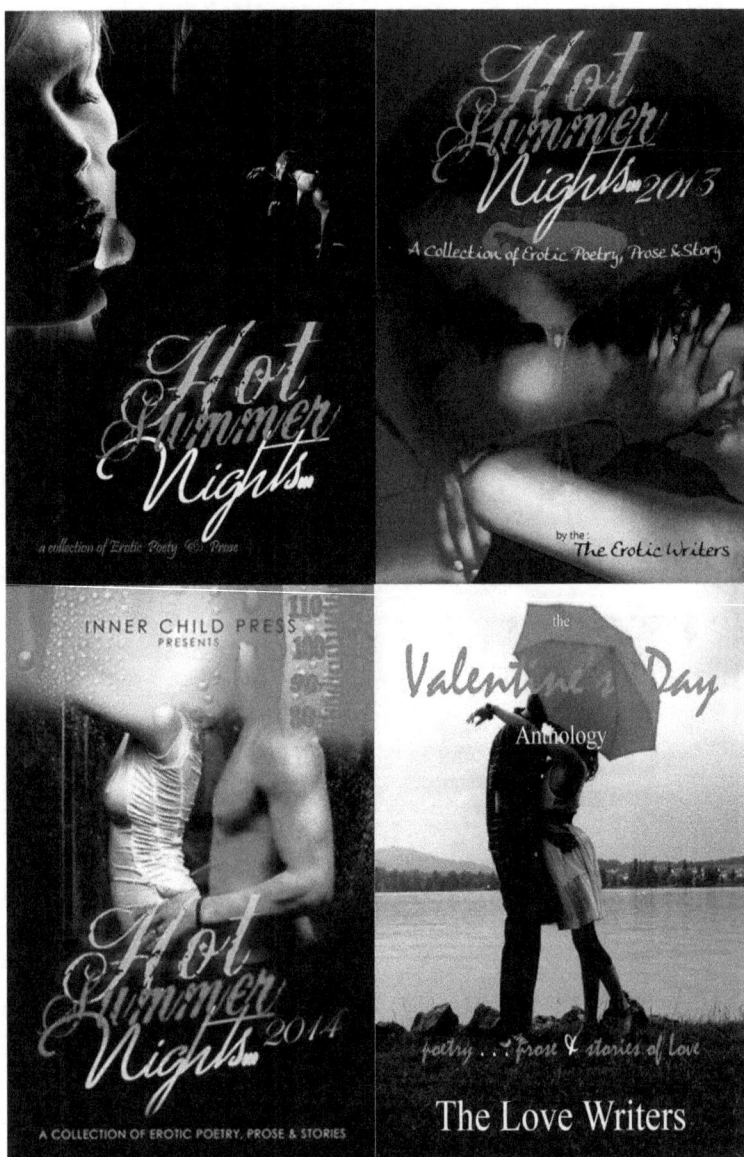

Now Available

www.innerchildpress.com/anthologies

Inner Child Press Anthologies

healing through words

Poetry ... Prose ... Prayer ... Stories

a
Poetically
Spoken
Anthology
volume 1
Collector's Edition

The Poetry Posse
Presents

an anthology
of

Love

The Poetry Posse 2016

Now Available

www.innerchildpress.com/anthologies

213

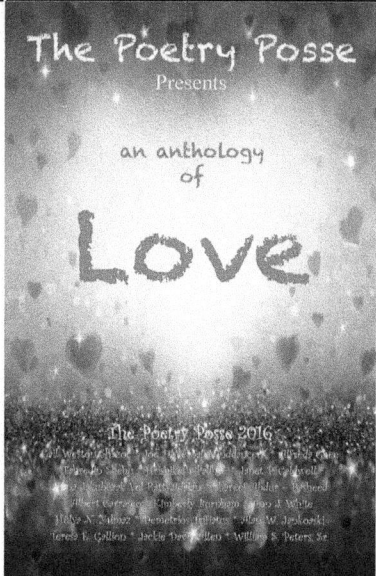

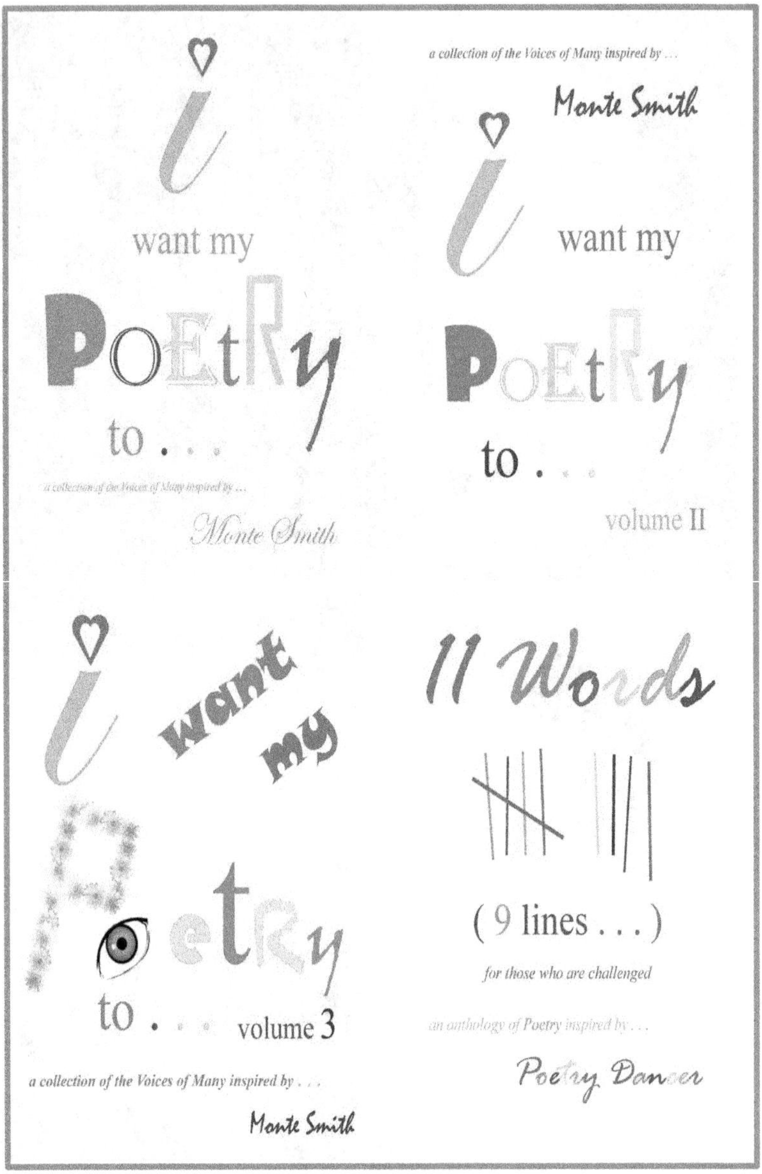

Now Available

www.innerchildpress.com/anthologies

The Year of the Poet
January 2014

The Poetry Posse

Jamie Bond
Gail Weston Shazor
Albert 'Infinite' Carrasco
Siddartha Beth Pierce
Janet P. Caldwell
June 'Bugg' Barefield
Debbie M. Allen
Tony Henninger
Joe DaVerbal Minddancer
Robert Gibbons
Neetu Wali
Shareef Abdur-Rasheed
William S. Peters, Sr.

Carnation

Our January Feature
Terri L. Johnson

the Year of the Poet
February 2014

violets

The Poetry Posse

Jamie Bond
Gail Weston Shazor
Albert 'Infinite' Carrasco
Siddartha Beth Pierce
Janet P. Caldwell
June 'Bugg' Barefield
Debbie M. Allen
Tony Henninger
Joe DaVerbal Minddancer
Robert Gibbons
Neetu Wali
Shareef Abdur-Rasheed
William S. Peters, Sr.

Our February Features
Teresa E. Gallion & Robert Gibson

the Year of the Poet
March 2014

The Poetry Posse

Jamie Bond
Gail Weston Shazor
Albert 'Infinite' Carrasco
Siddartha Beth Pierce
Janet P. Caldwell
June 'Bugg' Barefield
Debbie M. Allen
Tony Henninger
Joe DaVerbal Minddancer
Robert Gibbons
Neetu Wali
Shareef Abdur-Rasheed
Kimberly Burnham
William S. Peters, Sr.

daffodil

Our March Featured Poets
Alicia C. Cooper & hülya yılmaz

the Year of the Poet
April 2014

The Poetry Posse

Jamie Bond
Gail Weston Shazor
Albert 'Infinite' Carrasco
Siddartha Beth Pierce
Janet P. Caldwell
June 'Bugg' Barefield
Debbie M. Allen
Tony Henninger
Joe DaVerbal Minddancer
Robert Gibbons
Neetu Wali
Shareef Abdur-Rasheed
Kimberly Burnham
William S. Peters, Sr.

Our April Featured Poets
Fahredin Shehu
Martina Reisz Newberry
Justin Blackburn
Monte Smith

Sweet Pea

celebrating international poetry month

Now Available

www.innerchildpress.com/the-year-of-the-poet

215

Now Available

www.innerchildpress.com/the-year-of-the-poet

The Year of the Poet
September 2014

Aster — Morning-Glory

Wild Cosmos or September Birth Year Flower

September Feature Poets
Florence Malone * Keith Alan Hamilton

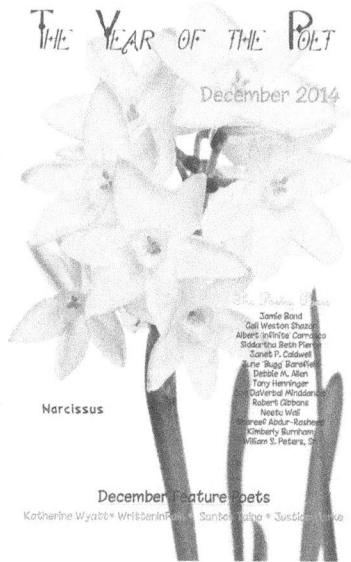

The Poetry Posse

Jamie Bond * Gail Weston Shazor * Albert 'InfiniTe' Carrasco * Siddartha Beth Pierce
Janet P. Caldwell * June 'Bugg' Barefield * Debbie M. Allen * Tony Henninger
Joe DaVerbal Minddancer * Robert Gibbons * Neetu Wali * Shareef Abdur-Rasheed
Kimberly Burnham * William S. Peters, Sr.

THE YEAR OF THE POET
October 2014

Red Poppy

The Poetry Posse
Jamie Bond * Gail Weston Shazor * Albert 'InfiniTe' Carrasco * Siddartha Beth Pierce
Janet P. Caldwell * June 'Bugg' Barefield * Debbie M. Allen * Tony Henninger
Joe DaVerbal Minddancer * Robert Gibbons * Neetu Wali * Shareef Abdur-Rasheed
Kimberly Burnham * William S. Peters, Sr.

October Feature Poets
Ceri Naz * Rajendra Padhi * Elizabeth Castillo

THE YEAR OF THE POET
November 2014

Chrysanthemum

The Poetry Posse
Jamie Bond * Gail Weston Shazor * Albert 'InfiniTe' Carrasco * Siddartha Beth Pierce
Janet P. Caldwell * June 'Bugg' Barefield * Debbie M. Allen * Tony Henninger
Joe DaVerbal Minddancer * Robert Gibbons * Neetu Wali * Shareef Abdur-Rasheed
Kimberly Burnham * William S. Peters, Sr.

November Feature Poets
Jocelyn Mosman * Jackie Allen * James Moore * Neville Hiatt

THE YEAR OF THE POET
December 2014

Narcissus

The Poetry Posse
Jamie Bond
Gail Weston Shazor
Albert 'InfiniTe' Carrasco
Siddartha Beth Pierce
Janet P. Caldwell
June 'Bugg' Barefield
Debbie M. Allen
Tony Henninger
DaVerbal Minddancer
Robert Gibbons
Neetu Wali
Shareef Abdur-Rasheed
Kimberly Burnham
William S. Peters, Sr.

December Feature Poets
Katherine Wyatt * WrittenInRed * Santosh Bakaya * Justice Once

Now Available
www.innerchildpress.com/the-year-of-the-poet

THE YEAR OF THE POET II

January 2015

Garnet

The Poetry Posse

Jamie Bond
Gail Weston Shazor
Albert 'Infinite' Carrasco
Siddartha Beth Pierce
Janet P. Caldwell
Tony Henninger
Joe DaVerbal Minddancer
Robert Gibbons
Neetu Wali
Shareef Abdur ~ Rasheed
Kimberly Burnham
Ann White
Keith Alan Hamilton
Katherine Wyatt
Fahredin Shehu
Hülya N. Yılmaz
Teresa E. Gallion
Jackie Allen
William S. Peters, Sr.

January Feature Poets
Bismay Mohanti * Jen Walls * Eric Judah

THE YEAR OF THE POET II

February 2015

Amethyst

THE POETRY POSSE

Jamie Bond
Gail Weston Shazor
Albert 'Infinite' Carrasco
Siddartha Beth Pierce
Janet P. Caldwell
Tony Henninger
Joe DaVerbal Minddancer
Robert Gibbons
Neetu Wali
Shareef Abdur ~ Rasheed
Kimberly Burnham
Ann White
Keith Alan Hamilton
Katherine Wyatt
Fahredin Shehu
Hülya N. Yılmaz
Teresa E. Gallion
Jackie Allen
William S. Peters, Sr.

FEBRUARY FEATURE POETS
Iram Fatima * Bob McNeil * Kerstin Centervall

The Year of the Poet II

March 2015

Our Featured Poets
Heung Sook * Anthony Arnold * Alicia Poland

Bloodstone

The Poetry Posse 2015
Jamie Bond * Gail Weston Shazor * Albert 'Infinite' Carrasco
Siddartha Beth Pierce * Janet P. Caldwell * Tony Henninger
Joe DaVerbal Minddancer * Neetu Wali * Shareef Abdur ~ Rasheed
Kimberly Burnham * Ann White * Keith Alan Hamilton
Katherine Wyatt * Fahredin Shehu * Hülya N. Yılmaz
Teresa E. Gallion * Jackie Allen * William S. Peters, Sr.

The Year of the Poet II

April 2015

Celebrating International Poetry Month

Our Featured Poets
Raja Williams * Dennis Ferado * Laure Charazac

Diamonds

The Poetry Posse 2015
Jamie Bond * Gail Weston Shazor * Albert 'Infinite' Carrasco
Siddartha Beth Pierce * Janet P. Caldwell * Tony Henninger
Joe DaVerbal Minddancer * Neetu Wali * Shareef Abdur ~ Rasheed
Kimberly Burnham * Ann White * Keith Alan Hamilton
Katherine Wyatt * Fahredin Shehu * Hülya N. Yılmaz
Teresa E. Gallion * Jackie Allen * William S. Peters, Sr.

Now Available

www.innerchildpress.com/the-year-of-the-poet

The Year of the Poet II
May 2015

May's Featured Poets

Geri Algeri
Akin Mosi Chinneru
Anna Jakubcza

Emeralds

The Poetry Posse 2015
Jamie Bond * Gail Weston Shazor * Albert 'Infinite' Carrasco
Siddartha Beth Pierce * Janet P. Caldwell * Tony Henninger
Joe DaVerbal Minddancer * Neetu Wali * Shareef Abdur – Rasheed
Kimberly Burnham * Ann White * Keith Alan Hamilton
Katherine Wyatt * Fahredin Shehu * Hülya N. Yılmaz
Teresa E. Gallion * Jackie Allen * William S. Peters, Sr.

The Year of the Poet II
June 2015

June's Featured Poets
Anahit Arustamyan * Yvette D. Marvell * Regina A. Walker

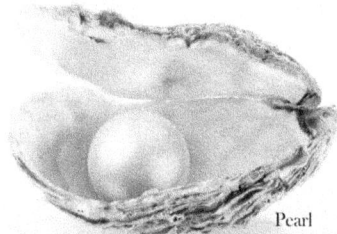

Pearl

The Poetry Posse 2015
Jamie Bond * Gail Weston Shazor * Albert 'Infinite' Carrasco
Siddartha Beth Pierce * Janet P. Caldwell * Tony Henninger
Joe DaVerbal Minddancer * Neetu Wali * Shareef Abdur – Rasheed
Kimberly Burnham * Ann White * Keith Alan Hamilton
Katherine Wyatt * Fahredin Shehu * Hülya N. Yılmaz
Teresa E. Gallion * Jackie Allen * William S. Peters, Sr.

The Year of the Poet II
July 2015

The Featured Poets for July 2015
Abhik Shome * Christina Neal * Robert Neal

Rubies

The Poetry Posse 2015
Jamie Bond * Gail Weston Shazor * Albert 'Infinite' Carrasco
Siddartha Beth Pierce * Janet P. Caldwell * Tony Henninger
Joe DaVerbal Minddancer * Neetu Wali * Shareef Abdur – Rasheed
Kimberly Burnham * Ann White * Keith Alan Hamilton
Katherine Wyatt * Fahredin Shehu * Hülya N. Yılmaz
Teresa E. Gallion * Jackie Allen * William S. Peters, Sr.

The Year of the Poet II
August 2015

Peridot

Featured Poets
Gayle Howell
Ann Chalasz
Christopher Schultz

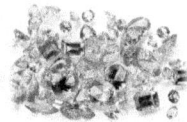

The Poetry Posse 2015
Jamie Bond * Gail Weston Shazor * Albert 'Infinite' Carrasco
Siddartha Beth Pierce * Janet P. Caldwell * Tony Henninger
Joe DaVerbal Minddancer * Neetu Wali * Shareef Abdur – Rasheed
Kimberly Burnham * Ann White * Keith Alan Hamilton
Katherine Wyatt * Fahredin Shehu * Hülya N. Yılmaz
Teresa E. Gallion * Jackie Allen * William S. Peters, Sr.

Now Available
www.innerchildpress.com/the-year-of-the-poet

The Year of the Poet II
September 2015

Featured Poets
Alfreda Ghee * Lonneice Weeks Badley * Demetrios Trifiatis

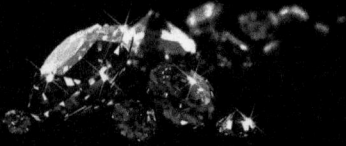

Sapphires

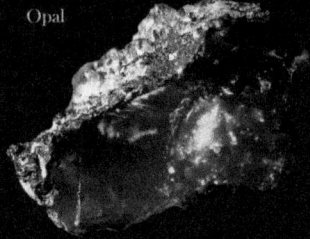

The Poetry Posse 2015

Jamie Bond * Gail Weston Shazor * Albert 'Infinite' Carrasco
Siddartha Beth Pierce * Janet P. Caldwell * Tony Henninger
Joe DaVerbal Minddancer * Neetu Wali * Shareef Abdur – Rasheed
Kimberly Burnham * Ann White * Keith Alan Hamilton
Katherine Wyatt * Fahredin Shehu * Hülya N. Yilmaz
Teresa E. Gallion * Jackie Allen * William S. Peters, Sr.

The Year of the Poet II
October 2015

Featured Poets
Monte Smith * Laura J. Wolfe * William Washington

Opal

The Poetry Posse 2015

Jamie Bond * Gail Weston Shazor * Albert 'Infinite' Carrasco
Siddartha Beth Pierce * Janet P. Caldwell * Tony Henninger
Joe DaVerbal Minddancer * Neetu Wali * Shareef Abdur – Rasheed
Kimberly Burnham * Ann White * Keith Alan Hamilton
Katherine Wyatt * Fahredin Shehu * Hülya N. Yilmaz
Teresa E. Gallion * Jackie Allen * William S. Peters, Sr.

The Year of the Poet II
November 2015

Featured Poets
Alan W. Jankowski
Bismay Mohanty
James Moore

Topaz

The Poetry Posse 2015

Jamie Bond * Gail Weston Shazor * Albert 'Infinite' Carrasco
Siddartha Beth Pierce * Janet P. Caldwell * Tony Henninger
Joe DaVerbal Minddancer * Neetu Wali * Shareef Abdur – Rasheed
Kimberly Burnham * Ann White * Keith Alan Hamilton
Katherine Wyatt * Fahredin Shehu * Hülya N. Yilmaz
Teresa E. Gallion * Jackie Allen * William S. Peters, Sr.

The Year of the Poet II
December 2015

Featured Poets
Kerione Bryan * Michelle Joan Barulich * Neville Hiatt

Turquoise

The Poetry Posse 2015

Jamie Bond * Gail Weston Shazor * Albert 'Infinite' Carrasco
Siddartha Beth Pierce * Janet P. Caldwell * Tony Henninger
Joe DaVerbal Minddancer * Neetu Wali * Shareef Abdur – Rasheed
Kimberly Burnham * Ann White * Keith Alan Hamilton
Katherine Wyatt * Fahredin Shehu * Hülya N. Yilmaz
Teresa E. Gallion * Jackie Allen * William S. Peters, Sr.

Now Available

www.innerchildpress.com/the-year-of-the-poet

220

The Year of the Poet III
January 2016

Featured Poets

Lana Joseph * Atom Cyrus Rush * Christena Williams

Dark-eyed Junco

The Poetry Posse 2016

The Year of the Poet III
February 2016

Featured Poets

Anthony Arnold
Anna Chidzo

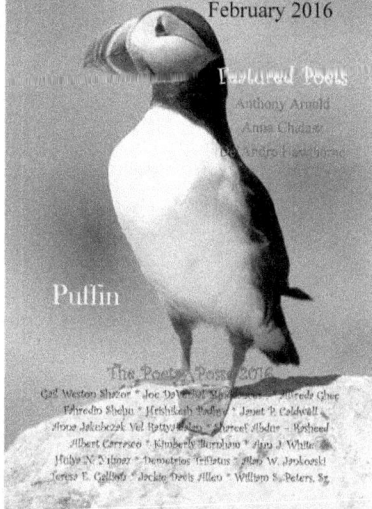

Puffin

The Poetry Posse 2016

The Year of the Poet
March 2016

Featured Poets

Jeton Kelmendi   Nizar Sartawi   Sami Muhanna

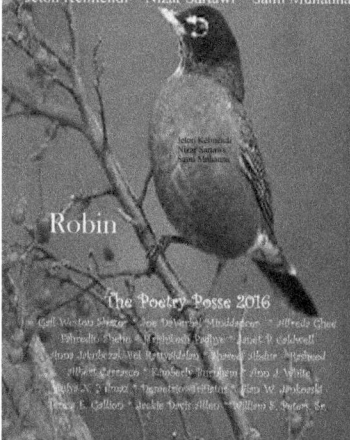

Robin

The Poetry Posse 2016

The Year of the Poet III

Featured Poets

Ali Abdolrezaei

Anna Chalasz

Agim Vinca

Ceri Naz

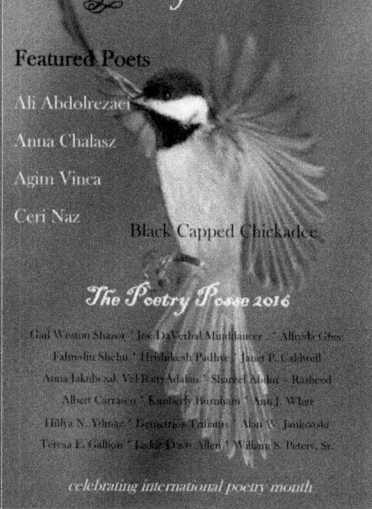

Black Capped Chickadee

The Poetry Posse 2016

celebrating international poetry month

Now Available

www.innerchildpress.com/the-year-of-the-poet

221

The Year of the Poet III
May 2016

Bob Strum
Barbara Allan
D.L. Davis

Oriole

The Year of the Poet III
June 2016

Featured Poets

Qibrije Demiri- Frangu
Naime Beqiraj
Faleeha Hassan
Bedri Zyberaj

Black Necked Stilt

The Poetry Posse 2016

The Year of the Poet III
July 2016

Featured Poets

Iram Fatima 'Ashi'
Langley Shazor
Jody Doty
Emilia T. Davis

Indigo Bunting

The Poetry Posse 2016

The Year of the Poet III
August 2016

Featured Poets

Anita Dash
Irena Jovanovic
Malgorzata Gouluda

Painted Bunting

The Poetry Posse 2016

Now Available

www.innerchildpress.com/the-year-of-the-poet

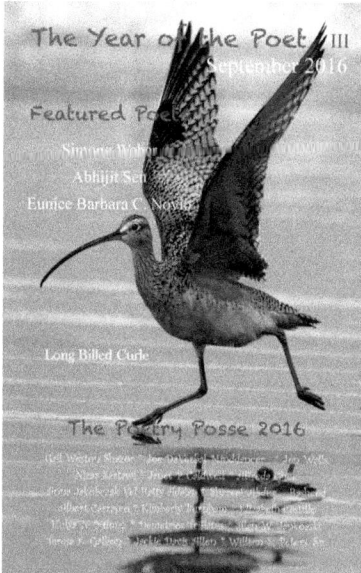

The Year of the Poet III
September 2016

Featured Poets

Simone Walter
Abhijit Sen
Eunice Barbara C. Novio

Long Billed Curle

The Poetry Posse 2016

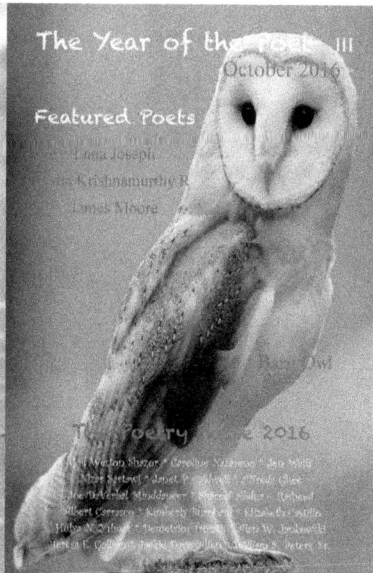

The Year of the Poet III
October 2016

Featured Poets

Uma Joseph
Sri Krishnamurthy R
James Moore

Barn Owl

The Poetry Posse 2016

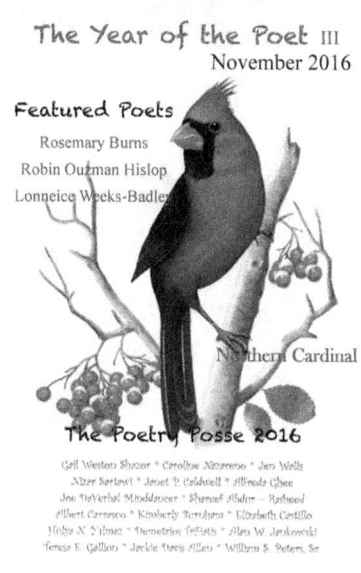

The Year of the Poet III
November 2016

Featured Poets

Rosemary Burns
Robin Ouzman Hislop
Lonneice Weeks-Badley

Northern Cardinal

The Poetry Posse 2016

Gail Weston Shazor * Caroline Nazareno * Jen Walls
Nizar Sartawi * Janet P. Caldwell * Alfreda Ghee
Joe DaVerbal Minddancer * Shareef Abdur — Rasheed
Albert Carrasco * Kimberly Burnham * Elizabeth Castillo
Hülya N. Yılmaz * Demetrios Trifiatis * Alan W. Jankowski
Teresa E. Gallion * Jackie Davis Allen * William S. Peters, Sr.

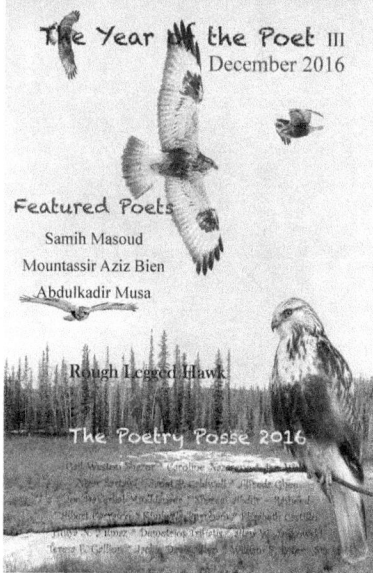

The Year of the Poet III
December 2016

Featured Poets

Samih Masoud
Mountassir Aziz Bien
Abdulkadir Musa

Rough Legged Hawk

The Poetry Posse 2016

Now Available

www.innerchildpress.com/the-year-of-the-poet

223

The Year of the Poet IV
January 2017

Featured Poets
Jon Winell
Natalie Shields
Irani Fatima Asdi

Quaking Aspen

The Poetry Posse 2017

Gail Weston Shazor * Caroline Nazareno * Bismay Mohanty
Nizar Sartawi * Jackie Jakubczak Val Batty Adolen * Jen Wells
Joe DaVerbal Minddancer * Shareef Abdur – Rasheed
Albert Carrasco * Kimberly Burnham * Elizabeth Castillo
Hülya N. Yılmaz * Telesha Hassan * Alan W. Jankowski
Teresa E. Gallion * Jackie Davis Allen * William S. Peters, Sr.

The Year of the Poet IV
February 2017

Featured Poets
Lin Ross
Sohkana Fathi
Oriel Gitani

Witch Hazel

The Poetry Posse 2017

Gail Weston Shazor * Caroline Nazareno * Bismay Mohanty
Nizar Sartawi * Jhona Jakubczak Val Batty Adolen * Jen Wells
Joe DaVerbal Minddancer * Shareef Abdur – Rasheed
Albert Carrasco * Kimberly Burnham * Elizabeth Castillo
Hülya N. Yılmaz * Telesha Hassan * Alan W. Jankowski
Teresa E. Gallion * Jackie Davis Allen * William S. Peters, Sr.

The Year of the Poet IV
March 2017

Featured Poets
Tremell Stevens
Francisca Ricinski
Jamil Abu Shaih

The Eastern Redbud

The Poetry Posse 2017

Gail Weston Shazor * Caroline Nazareno * Bismay Mohanty
Teresa E. Gallion * Jhona Jakubczak Val Batty Adolen
Joe DaVerbal Minddancer * Shareef Abdur – Rasheed
Albert Carrasco * Kimberly Burnham * Elizabeth Castillo
Hülya N. Yılmaz * Telesha Hassan * Jackie Davis Allen
Jen Wells * Nizar Sartawi * * William S. Peters, Sr.

The Year of the Poet IV
April 2017

Featured Poets
Dr. Ruchida Barman
Neptune Barman
Masood Khalaf

The Blossoming Cherry

The Poetry Posse 2017

Gail Weston Shazor * Caroline Nazareno * Bismay Mohanty
Teresa E. Gallion * Jhona Jakubczak Val Batty Adolen
Joe DaVerbal Minddancer * Shareef Abdur – Rasheed
Albert Carrasco * Kimberly Burnham * Elizabeth Castillo
Hülya N. Yılmaz * Telesha Hassan * Jackie Davis Allen
Jen Wells * Nizar Sartawi * * William S. Peters, Sr.

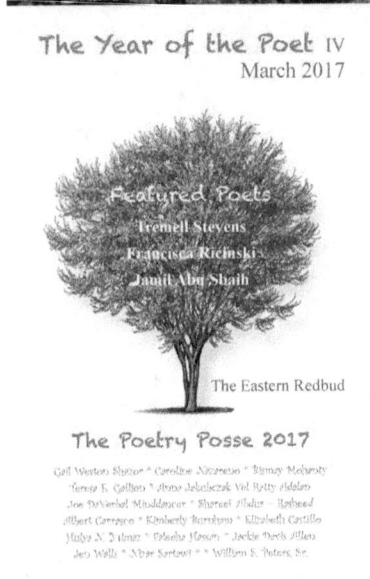

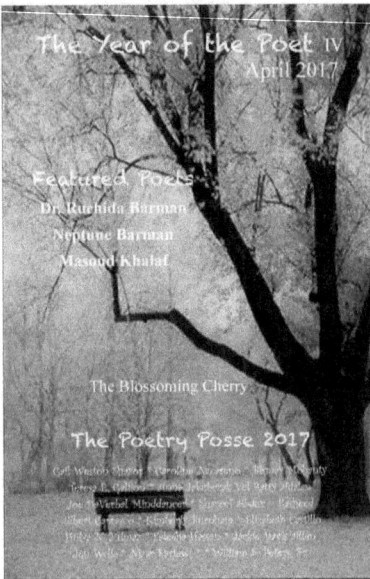

Now Available

www.innerchildpress.com/the-year-of-the-poet

The Year of the Poet IV
May 2017

The Flowering Dogwood Tree

Featured Poets
Kallisa Powell
Alicja Maria Kuberska
Fethi Sassi

The Poetry Posse 2017

Gail Weston Shazor * Caroline Nazareno * Bismay Mohanty
Teresa E. Gallion * Anna Jakubczak Vel Ratty Adalan
Joe DaVerbal Minddancer * Shareef Abdur – Rasheed
Albert Carrasco * Kimberly Burnham * Elizabeth Castillo
Hülya N. Yılmaz * Falguni Hasan * Jackie Davis Allen
Jen Walls * Nizar Sartawi * * William S. Peters, Sr.

The Year of the Poet IV
June 2017

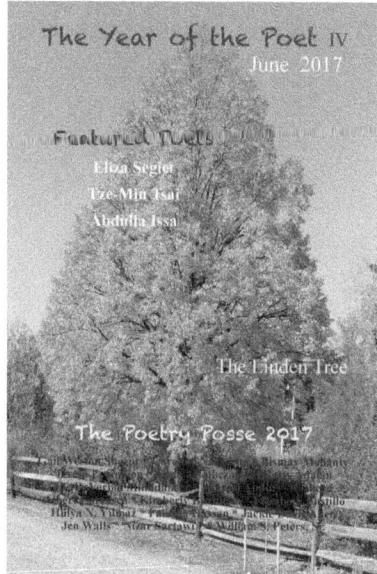

Featured Poets
Eliza Segiet
Tze-Min Tsai
Abdulla Issa

The Linden Tree

The Poetry Posse 2017

Gail Weston Shazor * Caroline Nazareno * Bismay Mohanty
Teresa E. Gallion * Anna Jakubczak Vel Ratty Adalan
Joe DaVerbal Minddancer * Shareef Abdur – Rasheed
Albert Carrasco * Kimberly Burnham * Elizabeth Castillo
Hülya N. Yılmaz * Falguni Hasan * Jackie Davis Allen
Jen Walls * Nizar Sartawi * * William S. Peters, Sr.

The Year of the Poet IV
July 2017

Featured Poets
Anca Mihaela Bruma
Ibaa Ismail
Zvonko Taneski

The Oak Moon

The Poetry Posse 2017

Gail Weston Shazor * Caroline Nazareno * Bismay Mohanty
Teresa E. Gallion * Anna Jakubczak Vel Ratty Adalan
Joe DaVerbal Minddancer * Shareef Abdur – Rasheed
Albert Carrasco * Kimberly Burnham * Elizabeth Castillo
Hülya N. Yılmaz * Falguni Hasan * Jackie Davis Allen
Jen Walls * Nizar Sartawi * * William S. Peters, Sr.

The Year of the Poet IV
August 2017

Featured Poets
Jonathan Aquino
Kitty Hsu
Langley Shazor

The Hazelnut Tree

The Poetry Posse 2017

Gail Weston Shazor * Caroline Nazareno *
Teresa E. Gallion * Anna Jakubczak Vel Ratty Adalan
Joe DaVerbal Minddancer * Shareef Abdur – Rasheed
Albert Carrasco * Kimberly Burnham * Elizabeth Castillo
Hülya N. Yılmaz * Falguni Hasan * Jackie Davis Allen
Jen Walls * Nizar Sartawi * * William S. Peters, Sr.

Now Available

www.innerchildpress.com/the-year-of-the-poet

The Year of the Poet IV
September 2017

Featured Poets

Martina Reisz Newber
Ameer Nassir
Christine Fulco Neal
Robert Neal

The Elm Tree

The Poetry Posse 2017

Gail Weston Shazor * Caroline Nazareno * Bismay Mohanty
Teresa E. Gallion * Anna Jakubczak Vel Ratty Adalan
Joe DaVerbal Minddancer * Shareef Abdur – Rasheed
Albert Carrasco * Kimberly Burnham * Elizabeth Castillo
Hülya N. Yılmaz * Faleeha Hassan * Jackie Davis Allen
Jen Walls * Nizar Sartawi * William S. Peters, Sr.

The Year of the Poet IV
October 2017

Featured Poets

Ahmed Abu Saleem
Nedal Al-Qaeim
Sadeddin Shahin

The Black Walnut Tree

The Poetry Posse 2017

Gail Weston Shazor * Caroline Nazareno * Bismay Mohanty
Teresa E. Gallion * Anna Jakubczak Vel Ratty Adalan
Joe DaVerbal Minddancer * Shareef Abdur – Rasheed
Albert Carrasco * Kimberly Burnham * Elizabeth Castillo
Hülya N. Yılmaz * Faleeha Hassan * Jackie Davis Allen
Jen Walls * Nizar Sartawi * * William S. Peters, Sr.

The Year of the Poet IV
November 2017

Featured Poets

Kay Peters
Alfreda D. Ghee
Gabriella Garofalo
Rosemary Cappello

The Tree of Life

The Poetry Posse 2017

Gail Weston Shazor * Caroline Nazareno * Bismay Mohanty
Teresa E. Gallion * Anna Jakubczak Vel Ratty Adalan
Joe DaVerbal Minddancer * Shareef Abdur – Rasheed
Albert Carrasco * Kimberly Burnham * Elizabeth Castillo
Hülya N. Yılmaz * Faleeha Hassan * Jackie Davis Allen
Jen Walls * Nizar Sartawi * William S. Peters, Sr.

The Year of the Poet IV
December 2017

Featured Poets

Justice Clarke
Mariel M. Pabroa
Kiley Brown

The Fig Tree

The Poetry Posse 2017

Gail Weston Shazor * Caroline Nazareno * Bismay Mohanty
Teresa E. Gallion * Anna Jakubczak Vel Ratty Adalan
Joe DaVerbal Minddancer * Shareef Abdur – Rasheed
Albert Carrasco * Kimberly Burnham * Elizabeth Castillo
Hülya N. Yılmaz * Faleeha Hassan * Jackie Davis Allen
Jen Walls * Nizar Sartawi * William S. Peters, Sr.

Now Available

www.innerchildpress.com/the-year-of-the-poet

The Year of the Poet V
January 2018
Featured Poets

Iyad Shamasnah

Yoomeun Hamuch

Ali Abdolrezaei

Aksum

The Poetry Posse 2018
Gail Weston Shazor * Caroline Nazareno * Tezmin Ition Tsai
Hülya N. Yılmaz * Faleeha Hassan * Jackie Davis Allen
Teresa E. Gallion * Anna Jakubczak Vel Ratty Adalan
Alicja Maria Kuberska * Shareef Abdur – Rasheed
Kimberly Burnham * Elizabeth Castillo
Nizar Sartawi * William S. Peters, Sr.

The Year of the Poet V
February 2018

Sabean

Featured Poets

Muhammad Azram

Anna Szawracka

Abhilipsa Kuanar

Aanika Aery

The Poetry Posse 2018
Gail Weston Shazor * Caroline Nazareno * Tezmin Ition Tsai
Hülya N. Yılmaz * Faleeha Hassan * Jackie Davis Allen
Teresa E. Gallion * Anna Jakubczak Vel Ratty Adalan
Alicja Maria Kuberska * Shareef Abdur – Rasheed
Kimberly Burnham * Elizabeth Castillo
Nizar Sartawi * William S. Peters, Sr.

The Year of the Poet V
March 2018

Featured Poets

Iram Fatima 'Ashi'
Cassandra Swan
Jaleel Khazaal
Sharia Zairun

Mexico   Cuba

Belize
Guatemala
El Salvador
Honduras Jamaica Haiti Dominican Republic
Nicaragua   Puerto Rico
Costa Rica
Panama

Caribbean
&
Middle America

Colombia

The Poetry Posse 2018
Gail Weston Shazor * Nizar Sartawi * Hülya N. Yılmaz
Jackie Davis Allen * Caroline 'Ceri' Nazareno
Alicja Maria Kuberska * Teresa E. Gallion
Faleeha Hassan * Shareef Abdur – Rasheed
Kimberly Burnham * Elizabeth Castillo
Tezmin Ition Tsai * William S. Peters, Sr.

The Year of the Poet V
April 2018

Featured Poets

The Nez Perce

The Poetry Posse 2018

Now Available
www.innerchildpress.com/the-year-of-the-poet

The Year of the Poet V
May 2018

Featured Poets

Zakty Carregui de Leon Jr.
Sylwia K. Malinowska
Lindita Ahmeti
Ofelia Prodan

The Sumerians

The Poetry Posse 2018

Gail Weston Shazor * Nizar Sartawi * Hülya N. Yilmaz
Jackie Davis Allen * Caroline 'Ceri' Nazareno
Alicja Maria Kuberska * Teresa E. Gallion
Kimberly Burnham * Shareef Abdur – Rasheed
Faleeha Hassan * Elizabeth Castillo * Swapna Behera
Tezmin Ition Tsai * William S. Peters, Sr.

The Year of the Poet V
June 2018

Featured Poets

Bilall Maliqi * Daim Miftari * Gojko Božović * Sofija Živković

The Paleo Indians

The Poetry Posse 2018

Gail Weston Shazor * Nizar Sartawi * Hülya N. Yilmaz
Jackie Davis Allen * Caroline 'Ceri' Nazareno
Alicja Maria Kuberska * Teresa E. Gallion
Kimberly Burnham * Shareef Abdur – Rasheed
Faleeha Hassan * Elizabeth Castillo * Swapna Behera
Tezmin Ition Tsai * William S. Peters, Sr.

The Year of the Poet V
July 2018

Featured Poets

Padmaja Iyengar-Paddy
Mohammad Ikbal Harb
Eliza Segiet
Tom Higgins

Oceania

The Poetry Posse 2018

Gail Weston Shazor * Nizar Sartawi * Hülya N. Yilmaz
Jackie Davis Allen * Caroline 'Ceri' Nazareno
Alicja Maria Kuberska * Teresa E. Gallion
Kimberly Burnham * Shareef Abdur – Rasheed
Faleeha Hassan * Elizabeth Castillo * Swapna Behera
Tezmin Ition Tsai * William S. Peters, Sr.

The Year of the Poet V
August 2018

Featured Poets

Hussein Habasch * Mircea Dan Duta * Naida Mujkić * Swagat Das

The Lapita

The Poetry Posse 2018

Gail Weston Shazor * Nizar Sartawi * Hülya N. Yilmaz
Jackie Davis Allen * Caroline 'Ceri' Nazareno
Alicja Maria Kuberska * Teresa E. Gallion
Kimberly Burnham * Shareef Abdur – Rasheed
Ashok K. Bhargava* Elizabeth Castillo * Swapna Behaera
Tezmin Ition Tsai * William S. Peters, Sr.

Now Available

www.innerchildpress.com/the-year-of-the-poet

The Year of the Poet V
September 2018

The Aztecs & Incas

Featured Poets
Kelinde Olaniyi-the Freedom
Eliza Segiet
Mackie Hassan Abdul Ghani
Lily Swarn

The Poetry Posse 2018
Gail Weston Shazor * Nizar Sartawi * Hülya N. Yılmaz
Jackie Davis Allen * Caroline 'Ceri' Nazareno
Alicja Maria Kuberska * Teresa E. Gallion
Kimberly Burnham * Shareef Abdur – Rasheed
Ashok K. Bhargava * Elizabeth Castillo * Swapna Behera
Tezmin Ition Tsai * William S. Peters, Sr.

The Year of the Poet V
October 2018

Featured Poets
Alicia Minjarez * Lonneice Weeks-Badley
Lopamudra Mishra * Abdelwahed Souayah

Bengali

The Poetry Posse 2018
Gail Weston Shazor * Nizar Sartawi * Hülya N. Yılmaz
Jackie Davis Allen * Caroline 'Ceri' Nazareno
Alicja Maria Kuberska * Teresa E. Gallion
Kimberly Burnham * Shareef Abdur – Rasheed
Ashok K. Bhargava * Elizabeth Castillo * Swapna Behera
Tezmin Ition Tsai * William S. Peters, Sr.

The Year of the Poet V
November 2018

Featured Poets
Michelle Joan Barulich * Monsif Beroual
Krystyna Konecka * Nassira Nezzar

The Poetry Posse 2018
Gail Weston Shazor * Nizar Sartawi * Hülya N. Yılmaz
Jackie Davis Allen * Caroline 'Ceri' Nazareno
Alicja Maria Kuberska * Teresa E. Gallion
Kimberly Burnham * Shareef Abdur – Rasheed
Ashok K. Bhargava * Elizabeth Castillo * Swapna Behera
Tezmin Ition Tsai * William S. Peters, Sr.

The Year of the Poet V
December 2018

Featured Poets
Rose Terranova Cirigliano
Joanna Kalinowska
Sokolović Emir
Dr. T. Ashok Chakravarthy

The Maori

The Poetry Posse 2018
Gail Weston Shazor * Nizar Sartawi * Hülya N. Yılmaz
Jackie Davis Allen * Caroline 'Ceri' Nazareno
Alicja Maria Kuberska * Teresa E. Gallion
Kimberly Burnham * Shareef Abdur – Rasheed
Ashok K. Bhargava * Elizabeth Castillo * Swapna Behera
Tezmin Ition Tsai * William S. Peters, Sr.

Now Available

www.innerchildpress.com/the-year-of-the-poet

229

The Year of the Poet VI

January 2019

Indigenous North Americans

Featured Poets

Houda Elfchtali
Anthony Briscoe
Iram Fatima 'Ashi'
Dr. K. K. Mathew

Dream Catcher

The Poetry Posse 2019

Gail Weston Shazor * Joe Paire * Hülya N. Yılmaz
Jackie Davis Allen * Caroline Ceri Nazareno
Alicja Maria Kubeńska * Teresa E. Gallion
Kimberly Burnham * Shareef Abdur – Rasheed
Ashok K. Bhargava * Elizabeth Castillo * Swapna Behera
Tezmin Ition Tsai * William S. Peters, Sr.

The Year of the Poet VI

February 2019

Featured Poets

Marek Łukaszewicz * Bharati Nayak
Aida G. Roque * Jean-Jacques Fournier

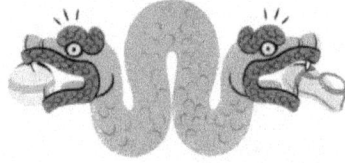

Meso–America

The Poetry Posse 2019

Gail Weston Shazor * Albert Carrasco * Hülya N. Yılmaz
Jackie Davis Allen * Caroline Nazareno * Eliza Segiet
Alicja Maria Kubeńska * Teresa E. Gallion * Joe Paire
Kimberly Burnham * Shareef Abdur – Rasheed
Ashok K. Bhargava * Elizabeth Castillo * Swapna Behera
Tezmin Ition Tsai * William S. Peters, Sr.

The Year of the Poet VI

March 2019

Featured Poets

Enesa Mahmić * Sylwia K. Malinowska
Shurouk Hammoud * Anwer Ghani

The Caribbean

The Poetry Posse 2019

Gail Weston Shazor * Albert Carrasco * Hülya N. Yılmaz
Jackie Davis Allen * Caroline Nazareno * Eliza Segiet
Alicja Maria Kubeńska * Teresa E. Gallion * Joe Paire
Kimberly Burnham * Shareef Abdur – Rasheed
Ashok K. Bhargava * Elizabeth Castillo * Swapna Behera
Tezmin Ition Tsai * William S. Peters, Sr.

The Year of the Poet VI

April 2019

Featured Poets

DL Davis * Michelle Joan Barulich
Lulëzim Haziri * Faleeha Hassan

Central & West Africa

The Poetry Posse 2019

Gail Weston Shazor * Albert Carrasco * Hülya N. Yılmaz
Jackie Davis Allen * Caroline Nazareno * Eliza Segiet
Alicja Maria Kubeńska * Teresa E. Gallion * Joe Paire
Kimberly Burnham * Shareef Abdur – Rasheed
Ashok K. Bhargava * Elizabeth Castillo * Swapna Behera
Tezmin Ition Tsai * William S. Peters, Sr.

Now Available

www.innerchildpress.com/the-year-of-the-poet

The Year of the Poet VI
May 2019

Featured Poets
Emad Al-Haydary * Hussein Nasser Jabr
Wahab Sherif * Abdul Razzaq Al Ameeri

Asia Southeast Asia and Maritime Asia

The Poetry Posse 2019
Gail Weston Shazor * Albert Carrasco * Hülya N. Yılmaz
Jackie Davis Allen * Caroline Nazareno * Eliza Segiet
Alicja Maria Kuberska * Teresa E. Gallion * Joe Paire
Kimberly Burnham * Shareef Abdur – Rasheed
Ashok K. Bhargava * Elizabeth Castillo * Swapna Behera
Tezmin Ition Tsai * William S. Peters, Sr.

The Year of the Poet VI
June 2019

Featured Poets
Kate Gandi Powlatanon * Balaj Babbar wili
Iwu Jeff * Mohamed Abdel Aziz Shmeis

Arctic
Circumpolar

The Poetry Posse 2019
Gail Weston Shazor * Albert Carrasco * Hülya N. Yılmaz
Jackie Davis Allen * Caroline Nazareno * Eliza Segiet
Alicja Maria Kuberska * Teresa E. Gallion * Joe Paire
Kimberly Burnham * Shareef Abdur – Rasheed
Ashok K. Bhargava * Elizabeth Castillo * Swapna Behera
Tezmin Ition Tsai * William S. Peters, Sr.

The Year of the Poet VI
July 2019

Featured Poets
Saadeddin Shahin   Andy Scott
Tabeedin Sheba   Alok Kumar Ray

The Horn of Africa

Ethiopia   Djibouti

Somalia   Eritrea

The Poetry Posse 2019
Gail Weston Shazor * Albert Carrasco * Hülya N. Yılmaz
Jackie Davis Allen * Caroline Nazareno * Eliza Segiet
Alicja Maria Kuberska * Teresa E. Gallion * Joe Paire
Kimberly Burnham * Shareef Abdur – Rasheed
Ashok K. Bhargava * Elizabeth Castillo * Swapna Behera
Tezmin Ition Tsai * William S. Peters, Sr.

The Year of the Poet VI
August 2019

Featured Poets
Shola Balogun * Bharati Nayak
Monalisa Dash Dwibedy * Mbizo Chirasha

Coexist

Southwest Asia

The Poetry Posse 2019
Gail Weston Shazor * Albert Carrasco * Hülya N. Yılmaz
Jackie Davis Allen * Caroline Nazareno * Eliza Segiet
Alicja Maria Kuberska * Teresa E. Gallion * Joe Paire
Kimberly Burnham * Shareef Abdur – Rasheed
Ashok K. Bhargava * Elizabeth Castillo * Swapna Behera
Tezmin Ition Tsai * William S. Peters, Sr.

Now Available
www.innerchildpress.com/the-year-of-the-poet

231

The Year of the Poet VI
September 2019

Featured Poets
Elena Liliana Popescu * Gobinda Biswas
Iram Fatima 'Ashi' * Joseph S. Spence, Sr.

The Caucasus
The Poetry Posse 2019

Gail Weston Shazor * Albert Carrasco * Hülya N. Yılmaz
Jackie Davis Allen * Caroline Nazareno * Eliza Segiet
Alicja Maria Kuberska * Teresa E. Gallion * Joe Paire
Kimberly Burnham * Shareef Abdur – Rasheed
Ashok K. Bhargava * Elizabeth Castillo * Swapna Behera
Tezmin Ition Tsai * William S. Peters, Sr.

The Year of the Poet VI
October 2019

Featured Poets
Ngozi Olivia Osuoha * Deusa Kondić
Pankhuri Sinha * Christena AV Williams

The Nile Valley
The Poetry Posse 2019

Gail Weston Shazor * Albert Carrasco * Hülya N. Yılmaz
Jackie Davis Allen * Caroline Nazareno * Eliza Segiet
Alicja Maria Kuberska * Teresa E. Gallion * Joe Paire
Kimberly Burnham * Shareef Abdur – Rasheed
Ashok K. Bhargava * Elizabeth Castillo * Swapna Behera
Tezmin Ition Tsai * William S. Peters, Sr.

The Year of the Poet VI
November 2019

Featured Poets
Rozalia Aleksandrova * Orbindu Ganga
Smruti Ranjan Mohanty * Sofia Skleida

Northern Asia
The Poetry Posse 2019

Gail Weston Shazor * Albert Carrasco * Hülya N. Yılmaz
Jackie Davis Allen * Caroline Nazareno * Eliza Segiet
Alicja Maria Kuberska * Teresa E. Gallion * Joe Paire
Kimberly Burnham * Shareef Abdur – Rasheed
Ashok K. Bhargava * Elizabeth Castillo * Swapna Behera
Tezmin Ition Tsai * William S. Peters, Sr.

The Year of the Poet VI
December 2019

Featured Poets
Robin Karim (Kumson) * Seqrie Paul
Bhajan Nayak * Kapardali D'Bidih

Oceania
The Poetry Posse 2019

Gail Weston Shazor * Albert Carrasco * Hülya N. Yılmaz
Jackie Davis Allen * Caroline Nazareno * Eliza Segiet
Alicja Maria Kuberska * Teresa E. Gallion * Joe Paire
Kimberly Burnham * Shareef Abdur – Rasheed
Ashok K. Bhargava * Elizabeth Castillo * Swapna Behera
Tezmin Ition Tsai * William S. Peters, Sr.

Now Available

www.innerchildpress.com/the-year-of-the-poet

The Year of the Poet VII
January 2020
Featured Poets
B S Tyagi * Ashok Chakravarthy Tholana
Anju Anna * Anwer Ghani

1901 Jean Henry Dunant and Frédéric Passy

The Year of Peace
Celebrating past Nobel Peace Prize Recipients

The Poetry Posse 2020
Gail Weston Shazor * Albert Carasco * Hülya N. Yılmaz
Jackie Davis Allen * Caroline Nazareno * Eliza Segiet
Alicja Maria Kuberska * Teresa E. Gallion * Joe Paire
Kimberly Burnham * Shareef Abdur – Rasheed
Ashok K. Bhargava * Elizabeth Castillo * Swapna Behera
Tezmin Ition Tsai * William S. Peters, Sr.

The Year of the Poet VII
February 2020
Featured Poets
Jennifer Adès * Martina Reisz Newberry
Ibrahim Honjo * Claudia Piccinno

Henri La Fontaine ~ 1913

The Year of Peace
Celebrating past Nobel Peace Prize Recipients

The Poetry Posse 2020
Gail Weston Shazor * Albert Carasco * Hülya N. Yılmaz
Jackie Davis Allen * Caroline Nazareno * Eliza Segiet
Alicja Maria Kuberska * Teresa E. Gallion * Joe Paire
Kimberly Burnham * Shareef Abdur – Rasheed
Ashok K. Bhargava * Elizabeth Castillo * Swapna Behera
Tezmin Ition Tsai * William S. Peters, Sr.

The Year of the Poet VII
March 2020
Featured Poets
Aziz Mountassir * Krishna Paraisa
Hannie Rouweler * Rozalia Aleksandrova

Aristide Briand ~ 1926 ~ Gustav Stresemann

The Year of Peace
Celebrating past Nobel Peace Prize Recipients

The Poetry Posse 2020
Gail Weston Shazor * Albert Carasco * Hülya N. Yılmaz
Jackie Davis Allen * Caroline Nazareno * Eliza Segiet
Alicja Maria Kuberska * Teresa E. Gallion * Joe Paire
Kimberly Burnham * Shareef Abdur – Rasheed
Ashok K. Bhargava * Elizabeth Castillo * Swapna Behera
Tezmin Ition Tsai * William S. Peters, Sr.

The Year of the Poet VII
April 2020
Featured Poets
Rohini Behera * Mircea Dan Duta
Monalisa Dash Dwibedy * NilavroNill Shoovro

Carlos Saavedra Lamas ~ 1936

The Year of Peace
Celebrating past Nobel Peace Prize Recipients

The Poetry Posse 2020
Gail Weston Shazor * Albert Carasco * Hülya N. Yılmaz
Jackie Davis Allen * Caroline Nazareno * Eliza Segiet
Alicja Maria Kuberska * Teresa E. Gallion * Joe Paire
Kimberly Burnham * Shareef Abdur – Rasheed
Ashok K. Bhargava * Elizabeth Castillo * Swapna Behera
Tezmin Ition Tsai * William S. Peters, Sr.

Now Available

www.innerchildpress.com/the-year-of-the-poet

The Year of the Poet VII
May 2020
Featured Poets
Alok Kumar Ray * Eden S. Trinidad
Franco Barbato * Izabela Zubko

Ralph Bunche ~ 1950

The Year of Peace
Celebrating past Nobel Peace Prize Recipients

The Poetry Posse 2020
Gail Weston Shazor * Albert Carassco * Hülya N. Yılmaz
Jackie Davis Allen * Caroline Nazareno * Eliza Segiet
Alicja Maria Kuberska * Teresa E. Gallion * Joe Paire
Kimberly Burnham * Shareef Abdur ~ Rasheed
Ashok K. Bhargava * Elizabeth Castillo * Swapna Behera
Tezmin Ition Tsai * William S. Peters, Sr.

The Year of the Poet VII
June 2020
Featured Poets
Eftichia Kapardeli * Metin Cengiz
Hussein Habasch * Kosh K Mathew

Albert John Lutuli ~ 1960

The Year of Peace
Celebrating past Nobel Peace Prize Recipients

The Poetry Posse 2020
Gail Weston Shazor * Albert Carassco * Hülya N. Yılmaz
Jackie Davis Allen * Caroline Nazareno * Eliza Segiet
Alicja Maria Kuberska * Teresa E. Gallion * Joe Paire
Kimberly Burnham * Shareef Abdur ~ Rasheed
Ashok K. Bhargava * Elizabeth Castillo * Swapna Behera
Tezmin Ition Tsai * William S. Peters, Sr.

The Year of the Poet VII
July 2020
Featured Poets
Mykola Martyniuk * Orbindu Ganga
Roula Pollard * Kam Praktisha

Norman Ernest Borlaug ~ 1970

The Year of Peace
Celebrating past Nobel Peace Prize Recipients

The Poetry Posse 2020
Gail Weston Shazor * Albert Carassco * Hülya N. Yılmaz
Jackie Davis Allen * Caroline Nazareno * Eliza Segiet
Alicja Maria Kuberska * Teresa E. Gallion * Joe Paire
Kimberly Burnham * Shareef Abdur ~ Rasheed
Ashok K. Bhargava * Elizabeth Castillo * Swapna Behera
Tezmin Ition Tsai * William S. Peters, Sr.

The Year of the Poet VII
August 2020
Featured Poets
Dr Pragya Suman * Chinh Nguyen
Srinivas Vasudev * Ugwu Leonard Ifeanyi, Jr.

Adolfo Pérez Esquivel ~ 1980

The Year of Peace
Celebrating past Nobel Peace Prize Recipients

The Poetry Posse 2020
Gail Weston Shazor * Albert Carassco * Hülya N. Yılmaz
Jackie Davis Allen * Caroline Nazareno * Eliza Segiet
Alicja Maria Kuberska * Teresa E. Gallion * Joe Paire
Kimberly Burnham * Shareef Abdur ~ Rasheed
Ashok K. Bhargava * Elizabeth Castillo * Swapna Behera
Tezmin Ition Tsai * William S. Peters, Sr.

Now Available

www.innerchildpress.com/the-year-of-the-poet

The Year of the Poet VII
September 2020
Featured Poets
Raed Anis Al-Jishi • Soikolovié Snežana
Dr. Brajesh Kumar Gupta • Omid Najafi

Mikhail Sergeyevich Gorbachev ~ 1990

The Year of Peace
Celebrating past Nobel Peace Prize Recipients

The Poetry Posse 2020
Gail Weston Shazor • Albert Carasco • Hülya N. Yılmaz
Jackie Davis Allen • Caroline Nazareno • Eliza Segiet
Alicja Maria Kuberska • Teresa E. Gallion • Joe Paire
Kimberly Burnham • Shareef Abdur – Rasheed
Ashok K. Bhargava • Elizabeth Castillo • Swapna Behera
Tezmin Ition Tsai • William S. Peters, Sr.

The Year of the Poet VII
October 2020
Featured Poets
Mahmud A. Shdifat • Galina Italyanskaya
Nadeem Fraz • Avril Tanya Meallem

Kim Dae-jung ~ 2000

The Year of Peace
Celebrating past Nobel Peace Prize Recipients

The Poetry Posse 2020
Gail Weston Shazor • Albert Carasco • Hülya N. Yılmaz
Jackie Davis Allen • Caroline Nazareno • Eliza Segiet
Alicja Maria Kuberska • Teresa E. Gallion • Joe Paire
Kimberly Burnham • Shareef Abdur – Rasheed
Ashok K. Bhargava • Elizabeth Castillo • Swapna Behera
Tezmin Ition Tsai • William S. Peters, Sr.

The Year of the Poet VII
November 2020
Featured Poets
Elisa Mascia • Sue Lindenberg McClelland
Hatif Janabi • Ivan Gaćina

Liu Xiaobo ~ 2010

The Year of Peace
Celebrating past Nobel Peace Prize Recipients

The Poetry Posse 2020
Gail Weston Shazor • Albert Carasco • Hülya N. Yılmaz
Jackie Davis Allen • Caroline Nazareno • Eliza Segiet
Alicja Maria Kuberska • Teresa E. Gallion • Joe Paire
Kimberly Burnham • Shareef Abdur – Rasheed
Ashok K. Bhargava • Elizabeth Castillo • Swapna Behera
Tezmin Ition Tsai • William S. Peters, Sr.

The Year of the Poet VII
December 2020
Featured Poets
Ratan Ghosh • Ibtisam Ibrahim Al-Asady
Brindha Vinodh • Selma Kopic

Abiy Ahmed Ali ~ 2019

The Year of Peace
Celebrating past Nobel Peace Prize Recipients

The Poetry Posse 2020
Gail Weston Shazor • Albert Carasco • Hülya N. Yılmaz
Jackie Davis Allen • Caroline Nazareno • Eliza Segiet
Alicja Maria Kuberska • Teresa E. Gallion • Joe Paire
Kimberly Burnham • Shareef Abdur – Rasheed
Ashok K. Bhargava • Elizabeth Castillo • Swapna Behera
Tezmin Ition Tsai • William S. Peters, Sr.

Now Available
www.innerchildpress.com/the-year-of-the-poet

The Year of the Poet VIII
January 2021

Featured Global Poets
Andrew Scott * Debaprasanna Biswas
Shakil Kalam * Changming Yuan

Banksy's The Girl with the Pierced Eardrum

Poetry ... Ekphrasticly Speaking
The Poetry Posse 2020

Gail Weston Shazor * Albert Carasco * Hülya N. Yılmaz
Jackie Davis Allen * Caroline Nazareno * Eliza Segiet
Alicja Maria Kuberska * Teresa E. Gallion * Joe Paire
Kimberly Burnham * Shareef Abdur – Rasheed
Ashok K. Bhargava * Elizabeth Castillo * Swapna Behera
Tezmin Ition Tsai * William S. Peters, Sr.

The Year of the Poet VIII
February 2021

Featured Global Poets
T. Ramesh Babu * Ruchida Barman
Neptune Barman * Faleeha Hassan

Emory Douglas : 1968 Olympics mural

Poetry ... Ekphrasticly Speaking
The Poetry Posse 2021

Gail Weston Shazor * Albert Carasco * Hülya N. Yılmaz
Jackie Davis Allen * Caroline Nazareno * Eliza Segiet
Alicja Maria Kuberska * Teresa E. Gallion * Joe Paire
Kimberly Burnham * Shareef Abdur – Rasheed
Ashok K. Bhargava * Elizabeth Castillo * Swapna Behera
Tezmin Ition Tsai * William S. Peters, Sr.

The Year of the Poet VIII
March 2021

Featured Global Poets
Claudia Piccinno * Mohammed Jabr
Luzviminda Rivera *Nigar Arif

Tatyana Fazlalizadeh

Poetry ... Ekphrasticly Speaking
The Poetry Posse 2021

Gail Weston Shazor * Albert Carasco * Hülya N. Yılmaz
Jackie Davis Allen * Caroline Nazareno * Eliza Segiet
Alicja Maria Kuberska * Teresa E. Gallion * Joe Paire
Kimberly Burnham * Shareef Abdur – Rasheed
Ashok K. Bhargava * Elizabeth Castillo * Swapna Behera
Tezmin Ition Tsai * William S. Peters, Sr.

The Year of the Poet VIII
April 2021

Featured Global Poets
Katarzyna Brus- Sawczuk * Anwesha Paul
Rozalia Aleksandrova * Shahid Abbas

Pablo O'Higgins

Poetry ... Ekphrasticly Speaking
The Poetry Posse 2021

Gail Weston Shazor * Albert Carasco * Hülya N. Yılmaz
Jackie Davis Allen * Caroline Nazareno * Eliza Segiet
Alicja Maria Kuberska * Teresa E. Gallion * Joe Paire
Kimberly Burnham * Shareef Abdur – Rasheed
Ashok K. Bhargava * Elizabeth Castillo * Swapna Behera
Tezmin Ition Tsai * William S. Peters, Sr.

Now Available
www.innerchildpress.com/the-year-of-the-poet

The Year of the Poet VIII
May 2021

Featured Global Poets
Paramita Mukherjee Mullick * Rose Zennino
Jaydeep Sarangi * Bismay Mohanty

Diego Rivera

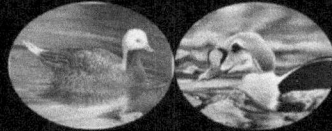

Poetry . . . Ekphrasticly Speaking
The Poetry Posse 2021

Gail Weston Shazor * Albert Carasco * Hülya N. Yılmaz
Jackie Davis Allen * Caroline Nazareno * Eliza Segiet
Alicja Maria Kuberska * Teresa E. Gallion * Joe Paire
Kimberly Burnham * Shareef Abdur – Rasheed
Ashok K. Bhargava * Elizabeth Castillo * Swapna Behera
Tezmin Ition Tsai * William S. Peters, Sr.

The Year of the Poet VIII
June 2021

Featured Global Poets
Alonzo 'JO' Gross * Lali Tsipi Michaeli
Tareq al Karmy * Tirthendu Ganguly

Rayen Kang

Poetry . . . Ekphrasticly Speaking
The Poetry Posse 2021

Gail Weston Shazor * Albert Carasco * Hülya N. Yılmaz
Jackie Davis Allen * Caroline Nazareno * Eliza Segiet
Alicja Maria Kuberska * Teresa E. Gallion * Joe Paire
Kimberly Burnham * Shareef Abdur – Rasheed
Ashok K. Bhargava * Elizabeth Castillo * Swapna Behera
Tezmin Ition Tsai * William S. Peters, Sr.

The Year of the Poet VIII
July 2021

Featured Global Poets
Iram Jaan * Vesna Mundishevska-Veljanovska
Ngozi Olivia Osuoha * Lan Qyqalla

Goncalao Mabunda

Poetry . . . Ekphrasticly Speaking
The Poetry Posse 2021

Gail Weston Shazor * Albert Carasco * Hülya N. Yılmaz
Jackie Davis Allen * Caroline Nazareno * Eliza Segiet
Alicja Maria Kuberska * Teresa E. Gallion * Joe Paire
Kimberly Burnham * Shareef Abdur – Rasheed
Ashok K. Bhargava * Elizabeth Castillo * Swapna Behera
Tezmin Ition Tsai * William S. Peters, Sr.

The Year of the Poet VIII
August 2021

Featured Global Poets
Caroline Laurent Turunc * Kamal Dhungana
Pankhuri Sinha * Paramita Mukherjee Mullick

Mundara Koorang

Poetry . . . Ekphrasticly Speaking
The Poetry Posse 2021

Gail Weston Shazor * Albert Carasco * Hülya N. Yılmaz
Jackie Davis Allen * Caroline Nazareno * Eliza Segiet
Alicja Maria Kuberska * Teresa E. Gallion * Joe Paire
Kimberly Burnham * Shareef Abdur – Rasheed
Ashok K. Bhargava * Elizabeth Castillo * Swapna Behera
Tezmin Ition Tsai * William S. Peters, Sr.

Now Available

www.innerchildpress.com/the-year-of-the-poet

The Year of the Poet VIII
September 2021
Featured Global Poets
Monsif Beroual * Sandesh Ghimire
Sharmila Poudel * Pavol Janik

Heather Jansch

Poetry ... Ekphrasticly Speaking

The Poetry Posse 2021

Gail Weston Shazor * Albert Carasco * Hülya N. Yılmaz
Jackie Davis Allen * Caroline Nazareno * Eliza Segiet
Alicja Maria Kuberska * Teresa E. Gallion * Joe Paire
Kimberly Burnham * Shareef Abdur – Rasheed
Ashok K. Bhargava * Elizabeth Castillo * Swapna Behera
Tezmin Ition Tsai * William S. Peters, Sr.

The Year of the Poet VIII
October 2021
Featured Global Poets
C. E. Shy * Saswata Ganguly
Suranjit Gain * Hasiba Hilal

Dale Lamphere

Poetry ... Ekphrasticly Speaking

The Poetry Posse 2021

Gail Weston Shazor * Albert Carasco * Hülya N. Yılmaz
Jackie Davis Allen * Caroline Nazareno * Eliza Segiet
Alicja Maria Kuberska * Teresa E. Gallion * Joe Paire
Kimberly Burnham * Shareef Abdur – Rasheed
Ashok K. Bhargava * Elizabeth Castillo * Swapna Behera
Tezmin Ition Tsai * William S. Peters, Sr.

The Year of the Poet VIII
November 2021
Featured Global Poets
Errol D. Bean * Ibrahim Honjo
Tanja Ajtic * Rajashree Mohapatra

Andy Goldsworthy

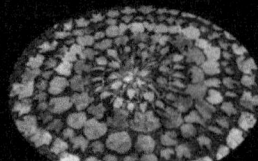

Poetry ... Ekphrasticly Speaking

The Poetry Posse 2021

Gail Weston Shazor * Albert Carasco * Hülya N. Yılmaz
Jackie Davis Allen * Caroline Nazareno * Eliza Segiet
Alicja Maria Kuberska * Teresa E. Gallion * Joe Paire
Kimberly Burnham * Shareef Abdur – Rasheed
Ashok K. Bhargava * Elizabeth Castillo * Swapna Behera
Tezmin Ition Tsai * William S. Peters, Sr.

The Year of the Poet VIII
December 2021
Featured Global Poets
Orbinda Ganga * Fadairo Tesleem
Anthony Arnold * Iyad Shamasnah

Fredric Edwin Church

Poetry ... Ekphrasticly Speaking

The Poetry Posse 2021

Gail Weston Shazor * Albert Carasco * Hülya N. Yılmaz
Jackie Davis Allen * Caroline Nazareno * Eliza Segiet
Alicja Maria Kuberska * Teresa E. Gallion * Joe Paire
Kimberly Burnham * Shareef Abdur – Rasheed
Ashok K. Bhargava * Elizabeth Castillo * Swapna Behera
Tezmin Ition Tsai * William S. Peters, Sr.

Now Available

www.innerchildpress.com/the-year-of-the-poet

238

The Year of the Poet IX
January 2022

Featured Global Poets
Ratan Ghosh * **Christine Neil-Wright**
Andrew Scott * **Ashok Kumar**

Climate Change : The Ice Cap

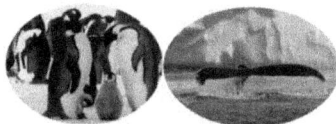

Poetry . . . Ekphrasticly Speaking

The Poetry Posse 2021

Gail Weston Shazor * Albert Carasco * Hülya N. Yılmaz
Jackie Davis Allen * Caroline Nazareno * Eliza Segiet
Alicja Maria Kuberska * Teresa E. Gallion * Joe Paire
Kimberly Burnham * Shareef Abdur – Rasheed
Ashok K. Bhargava * Elizabeth Castillo * Swapna Behera
Tezmin Ition Tsai * William S. Peters, Sr.

The Year of the Poet IX
February 2022

Featured Global Poets
Buza Buyanova * Ramón de Jesús Núñez Duval
Mammad Ismayil * Tarana Turan Rahimli

Climate Change and Mountains

Poetry . . . Ekphrasticly Speaking

The Poetry Posse 2021

Gail Weston Shazor * Albert Carasco * Hülya N. Yılmaz
Jackie Davis Allen * Caroline Nazareno * Eliza Segiet
Alicja Maria Kuberska * Teresa E. Gallion * Joe Paire
Kimberly Burnham * Shareef Abdur – Rasheed
Ashok K. Bhargava * Elizabeth Castillo * Swapna Behera
Tezmin Ition Tsai * William S. Peters, Sr.

The Year of the Poet IX
March 2022

Featured Global Poets
Dimitris P. Kraniotis * Marlene Pasini
Kennedy Ochieng * Swayam Prashant

Climate Change and Space Debris

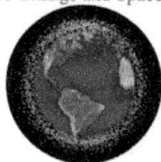

Poetry . . . Ekphrasticly Speaking

The Poetry Posse 2021

Gail Weston Shazor * Albert Carasco * Hülya N. Yılmaz
Jackie Davis Allen * Caroline Nazareno * Eliza Segiet
Alicja Maria Kuberska * Teresa E. Gallion * Joe Paire
Kimberly Burnham * Shareef Abdur – Rasheed
Ashok K. Bhargava * Elizabeth Castillo * Swapna Behera
Tezmin Ition Tsai * William S. Peters, Sr.

The Year of the Poet IX
April 2022

Featured Global Poets
Alonzo Gross * Dr. Debaprasanna Biswas
Monsif Beroual * Carol Aronoff

Climate Change and Oceans

*Celebrating our 100th Edition *

Poetry . . . Ekphrasticly Speaking

The Poetry Posse 2021

Gail Weston Shazor * Albert Carasco * Hülya N. Yılmaz
Jackie Davis Allen * Caroline Nazareno * Eliza Segiet
Alicja Maria Kuberska * Teresa E. Gallion * Joe Paire
Kimberly Burnham * Shareef Abdur – Rasheed
Ashok K. Bhargava * Elizabeth Castillo * Swapna Behera
Tezmin Ition Tsai * William S. Peters, Sr.

Now Available
www.innerchildpress.com/the-year-of-the-poet

The Year of the Poet IX
May 2022

Featured Global Poets

Ndaba Sibanda * Smrutiranjan Mohanty
Ajanta Paul * Monalisa Dash Dwibedy

Climate Change and Birds

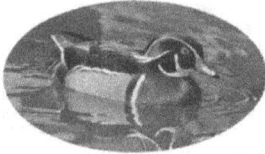

Poetry . . . Ekphrasticly Speaking

The Poetry Posse 2021

Gail Weston Shazor * Albert Carassco * Hülya N. Yılmaz
Jackie Davis Allen * Caroline Nazareno * Eliza Segiet
Alicja Maria Kuberska * Teresa E. Gallion * Joe Paire
Kimberly Burnham * Shareef Abdur – Rasheed
Ashok K. Bhargava * Elizabeth Castillo * Swapna Behera
Tezmin Ition Tsai * William S. Peters, Sr.

The Year of the Poet IX
June 2022

Featured Global Poets

Yuan Changming * Azeezat Okunlola
Tanja Ajtić * Philip Chijioke Abonyi

Climate Change and Trees

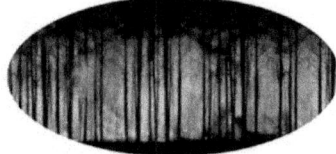

Poetry . . . Ekphrasticly Speaking

The Poetry Posse 2022

Gail Weston Shazor * Albert Carassco * Hülya N. Yılmaz
Jackie Davis Allen * Caroline Nazareno * Eliza Segiet
Alicja Maria Kuberska * Teresa E. Gallion * Joe Paire
Kimberly Burnham * Shareef Abdur – Rasheed
Ashok K. Bhargava * Elizabeth Castillo * Swapna Behera
Tezmin Ition Tsai * William S. Peters, Sr.

The Year of the Poet IX
July 2022

Featured Global Poets

Michelle Joan Barulich * Mili Das
Anna Ferriero * Ujjal Mandal

Climate Change and Animals

Poetry . . . Ekphrasticly Speaking

The Poetry Posse 2022

Gail Weston Shazor * Albert Carassco * Hülya N. Yılmaz
Jackie Davis Allen * Caroline Nazareno * Eliza Segiet
Alicja Maria Kuberska * Teresa E. Gallion * Joe Paire
Kimberly Burnham * Shareef Abdur – Rasheed
Ashok K. Bhargava * Elizabeth Castillo * Swapna Behera
Tezmin Ition Tsai * William S. Peters, Sr.

The Year of the Poet IX
August 2022

Featured Global Poets

Pankhuri Sinha * Abdulloh Abdumominov
Caroline Turunç * Tali Cohen Shabtai

Climate Change and Agriculture

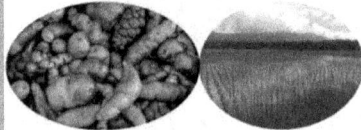

Poetry . . . Ekphrasticly Speaking

The Poetry Posse 2022

Gail Weston Shazor * Albert Carassco * Hülya N. Yılmaz
Jackie Davis Allen * Caroline Nazareno * Eliza Segiet
Alicja Maria Kuberska * Teresa E. Gallion * Joe Paire
Kimberly Burnham * Shareef Abdur – Rasheed
Ashok K. Bhargava * Elizabeth Castillo * Swapna Behera
Tezmin Ition Tsai * William S. Peters, Sr.

Now Available

www.innerchildpress.com/the-year-of-the-poet

The Year of the Poet IX
September 2022

Featured Global Poets
Ngozi Olivia Osuoha * Biswajit Mishra
Sylwia K. Malinowska * Sajid Hussein

Climate Change and Wind and Weather Patterns

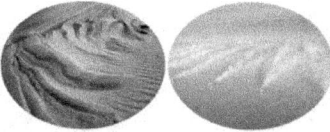

Poetry . . . Ekphrasticly Speaking

The Poetry Posse 2022

Gail Weston Shazor * Albert Carasco * Hülya N. Yılmaz
Jackie Davis Allen * Caroline Nazareno * Eliza Segiet
Alicja Maria Kubeńska * Teresa E. Gallion * Joe Paire
Kimberly Burnham * Shareef Abdur – Rasheed
Ashok K. Bhargava * Elizabeth Castillo * Swapna Behera
Tezmin Ition Tsai * William S. Peters, Sr.

The Year of the Poet IX
October 2022

Featured Global Poets
Andrew Kouroupos * Brenda Mohammed
Carthornia Kouroupos * Faleeha Hassan

Climate Change and Oil and Power

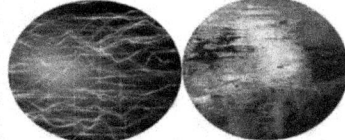

Poetry . . . Ekphrasticly Speaking

The Poetry Posse 2022

Gail Weston Shazor * Albert Carasco * Hülya N. Yılmaz
Jackie Davis Allen * Caroline Nazareno * Eliza Segiet
Alicja Maria Kubeńska * Teresa E. Gallion * Joe Paire
Kimberly Burnham * Shareef Abdur – Rasheed
Ashok K. Bhargava * Elizabeth Castillo * Swapna Behera
Tezmin Ition Tsai * William S. Peters, Sr.

The Year of the Poet IX
November 2022

Featured Global Poets
Hema Ravi * Shafkat Aziz Hajam
Selma Kopic * Ibrahim Honjo

Climate Change : Time to Act

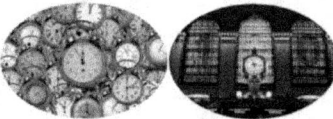

Poetry . . . Ekphrasticly Speaking

The Poetry Posse 2022

Gail Weston Shazor * Albert Carasco * Hülya N. Yılmaz
Jackie Davis Allen * Caroline Nazareno * Eliza Segiet
Alicja Maria Kubeńska * Teresa E. Gallion * Joe Paire
Kimberly Burnham * Shareef Abdur – Rasheed
Ashok K. Bhargava * Elizabeth Castillo * Swapna Behera
Tezmin Ition Tsai * William S. Peters, Sr.

The Year of the Poet IX
December 2022

Featured Global Poets
Elarbi Abdelfattah * Lorraine Cragg
Neha Bhandarkar * Robert Gibbons

Climate Change Bees, Butterflies and Insect life

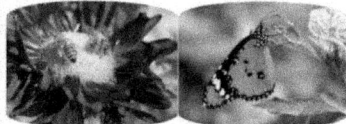

Poetry . . . Ekphrasticly Speaking

The Poetry Posse 2022

Gail Weston Shazor * Albert Carasco * Hülya N. Yılmaz
Jackie Davis Allen * Caroline Nazareno * Eliza Segiet
Alicja Maria Kubeńska * Teresa E. Gallion * Joe Paire
Kimberly Burnham * Shareef Abdur – Rasheed
Ashok K. Bhargava * Elizabeth Castillo * Swapna Behera
Tezmin Ition Tsai * William S. Peters, Sr.

Now Available

www.innerchildpress.com/the-year-of-the-poet

The Year of the Poet X
January 2023

Featured Global Poets

JuNe Barefield * Swayam Prashant
Willow Rose * Shabbirhusein K Jamnagerwalla

Children : Difference Makers

Iqbal Masih

The Poetry Posse 2023

Gail Weston Shazor * Albert Carasco * Hülya N. Yilmaz
Jackie Davis Allen * Caroline Nazareno * Kimberly Burnham
Alicja Maria Kuberska * Teresa E. Gallion * Joe Paire
Michelle Joan Barulich * Shareef Abdur - Rasheed
Ashok K. Bhargava * Elizabeth Castillo * Swapna Behera
Tezmin Ition Tsai * Eliza Segiet * William S. Peters, Sr.

The Year of the Poet X
February 2023

Featured Global Poets

Christena Williams * Hilda Graciela Kraft
Francesco Favetta * Dr. H.C. Louise Hudon

Children : Difference Makers

Ruby Bridges

The Poetry Posse 2023

Gail Weston Shazor * Albert Carasco * Hülya N. Yilmaz
Jackie Davis Allen * Caroline Nazareno * Kimberly Burnham
Alicja Maria Kuberska * Teresa E. Gallion * Joe Paire
Michelle Joan Barulich * Shareef Abdur - Rasheed
Ashok K. Bhargava * Elizabeth Castillo * Swapna Behera
Tezmin Ition Tsai * Eliza Segiet * William S. Peters, Sr.

The Year of the Poet X
March 2023

Featured Global Poets

Clarena Martínez Turizo * Binod Dawadi
Til Kumari Sharma * Petrouchka Alexieva

Children : Difference Makers

Yo Yo Ma

The Poetry Posse 2023

Gail Weston Shazor * Albert Carasco * Hülya N. Yilmaz
Jackie Davis Allen * Caroline Nazareno * Kimberly Burnham
Alicja Maria Kuberska * Teresa E. Gallion * Joe Paire
Michelle Joan Barulich * Shareef Abdur - Rasheed
Ashok K. Bhargava * Elizabeth Castillo * Swapna Behera
Tezmin Ition Tsai * Eliza Segiet * William S. Peters, Sr.

The Year of the Poet X
April 2023

Featured Global Poets

Maxwanette A Poetess * Alonzo Gross
Türkan Ergör * Ibrahim Honjo

Children : Difference Makers

Claudette Colvin

The Poetry Posse 2023

Gail Weston Shazor * Albert Carasco * Hülya N. Yilmaz
Jackie Davis Allen * Caroline Nazareno * Kimberly Burnham
Alicja Maria Kuberska * Teresa E. Gallion * Joe Paire
Michelle Joan Barulich * Shareef Abdur - Rasheed
Ashok K. Bhargava * Elizabeth Castillo * Swapna Behera
Tezmin Ition Tsai * Eliza Segiet * William S. Peters, Sr.

Now Available

www.innerchildpress.com/the-year-of-the-poet

The Year of the Poet X
May 2023

Csp Shrivastava * Michael Lee Johnson
Taghrid Bou Merhi * Yumnin Dhowa

Children : Difference Makers

Louis Braille
The Poetry Posse 2023

Gail Weston Shazor * Albert Carasco * Hülya N. Yilmaz
Jackie Davis Allen * Caroline Nazareno * Kimberly Burnham
Alicja Maria Kuberska * Teresa E. Gallion * Joe Paire
Michelle Joan Barulich * Shareef Abdur – Rasheed
Ashok K. Bhargava * Elizabeth Castillo * Swapna Behera
Tezmin Ition Tsai * Eliza Segiet * William S. Peters, Sr.

The Year of the Poet X
June 2023

Featured Global Poets

Kay Peters   Carthornia Kouroupos
Andrea Houroupos   Fateeha Hassan

Children : Difference Makers

Ryan Hreljac
The Poetry Posse 2023

The Year of the Poet X
July 2023

Featured Global Poets

Rajashree Mohapatra * Biswajit Mishra
Johan Karlsson * Teodozja Swiderska

Children : Difference Makers

~ Bana al-Abed ~
The Poetry Posse 2023

Gail Weston Shazor * Albert Carasco * Hülya N. Yilmaz
Jackie Davis Allen * Caroline Nazareno * Kimberly Burnham
Alicja Maria Kuberska * Teresa E. Gallion * Joe Paire
Michelle Joan Barulich * Shareef Abdur – Rasheed
Ashok K. Bhargava * Elizabeth Castillo * Swapna Behera
Tezmin Ition Tsai * Eliza Segiet * William S. Peters, Sr.

The Year of the Poet X
August 2023

Featured Global Poets

Kennedy Wanda Ochieng * Jose Lopez
Sylwia K. Malinowska * Laurent Grison

Children : Difference Makers

~ Kelvin Doe ~
The Poetry Posse 2023

Gail Weston Shazor * Albert Carasco * Hülya N. Yilmaz
Jackie Davis Allen * Caroline Nazareno * Kimberly Burnham
Alicja Maria Kuberska * Teresa E. Gallion * Joe Paire
Michelle Joan Barulich * Shareef Abdur – Rasheed
Ashok K. Bhargava * Elizabeth Castillo * Swapna Behera
Tezmin Ition Tsai * Eliza Segiet * William S. Peters, Sr.

Now Available

www.innerchildpress.com/the-year-of-the-poet

The Year of the Poet X
September 2023

Featured Global Poets
Eftichia Karpadeli * Chinh Nguyen
Nigar Agalarova * Carmela Cueva

Children : Difference Makers

~ Easton LaChappelle ~

The Poetry Posse 2023

Gail Weston Shazor * Albert Carasco * Hülya N. Yılmaz
Jackie Davis Allen * Caroline Nazareno * Kimberly Burnham
Alicja Maria Kuberska * Teresa E. Gallion * Joe Paire
Michelle Joan Barulich * Shareef Abdur – Rasheed
Ashok K. Bhargava * Elizabeth Castillo * Swapna Behera
Tezmin Ition Tsai * Eliza Segiet * William S. Peters, Sr.

The Year of the Poet X
October 2023

Featured Global Poets
CSP Shrivastava * Huniie Parker
Noreen Snyder * Ramkrishna Paul

Children : Difference Makers

~ Malala Yousafzai ~

The Poetry Posse 2023

Gail Weston Shazor * Albert Carasco * Hülya N. Yılmaz
Jackie Davis Allen * Caroline Nazareno * Kimberly Burnham
Alicja Maria Kuberska * Teresa E. Gallion * Joe Paire
Michelle Joan Barulich * Shareef Abdur – Rasheed
Ashok K. Bhargava * Elizabeth Castillo * Swapna Behera
Tezmin Ition Tsai * Eliza Segiet * William S. Peters, Sr.

The Year of the Poet X
November 2023

Featured Global Poets
Ibrahim Honjo * Balachandran Nair
Xanthi Hondrou-Hil * Francesco Favetta

Children : Difference Makers

~ Jean-Michel Basquiat ~

The Poetry Posse 2023

Gail Weston Shazor * Albert Carasco * Hülya N. Yılmaz
Jackie Davis Allen * Caroline Nazareno * Kimberly Burnham
Alicja Maria Kuberska * Teresa E. Gallion * Joe Paire
Michelle Joan Barulich * Shareef Abdur – Rasheed
Ashok K. Bhargava * Elizabeth Castillo * Swapna Behera
Tezmin Ition Tsai * Eliza Segiet * William S. Peters, Sr.

The Year of the Poet X
December 2023

Featured Global Poets
Caroline Laurent Turunc * Neha Bhandarkar
Shafkat Aziz Hajam * Elarbi Abdelfattah

Children : Difference Makers

~ Melati and Isabel Wijsen ~

The Poetry Posse 2023

Gail Weston Shazor * Albert Carasco * Hülya N. Yılmaz
Jackie Davis Allen * Caroline Nazareno * Kimberly Burnham
Alicja Maria Kuberska * Teresa E. Gallion * Joe Paire
Michelle Joan Barulich * Shareef Abdur – Rasheed
Ashok K. Bhargava * Elizabeth Castillo * Swapna Behera
Tezmin Ition Tsai * Eliza Segiet * William S. Peters, Sr.

Now Available

www.innerchildpress.com/the-year-of-the-poet

The Year of the Poet XI
January 2024

Featured Global Poets

Til Kumari Sharma * Shafkat Aziz Hajam
Daniela Marian * Eleni Vareilieu ... Auteuukoii

Renowned Poets

~ Phyllis Wheatley ~

The Poetry Posse 2024

Gail Weston Shazor * Albert Carasco * Hülya N. Yılmaz
Jackie Davis Allen * Caroline Nazareno * Mutawaf Shaheed
Alicja Maria Kuberska * Teresa E. Gallion * Noreen Snyder
Michelle Joan Barulich * Shareef Abdur – Rasheed
Ashok K. Bhargava * Elizabeth Castillo * Swapna Behera
Tezmin Ition Tsai * Eliza Segiet * William S. Peters, Sr.

The Year of the Poet XI
February 2024

Featured Global Poets

Caroline Laurent Turunç * Julia Payanetti
Lidia Chiarelli * Lina Buividavičiūtė

Renowned Poets

~ Omar Khayyam ~

The Poetry Posse 2024

Gail Weston Shazor * Albert Carasco * Hülya N. Yılmaz
Jackie Davis Allen * Caroline Nazareno * Mutawaf Shaheed
Alicja Maria Kuberska * Teresa E. Gallion * Noreen Snyder
Michelle Joan Barulich * Shareef Abdur – Rasheed
Ashok K. Bhargava * Elizabeth Castillo * Swapna Behera
Tezmin Ition Tsai * Eliza Segiet * William S. Peters, Sr.

The Year of the Poet XI
March 2024

Featured Global Poets

Francesco Favetta * Jagjit Singh Zandu
Carmela Núñez Yukimura Peruana * Michael Lee Johnson

Renowned Poets

~ Nâzim Hikmet ~

The Poetry Posse 2024

Gail Weston Shazor * Albert Carasco * Hülya N. Yılmaz
Jackie Davis Allen * Caroline Nazareno * Mutawaf Shaheed
Alicja Maria Kuberska * Teresa E. Gallion * Noreen Snyder
Michelle Joan Barulich * Shareef Abdur – Rasheed
Ashok K. Bhargava * Elizabeth Castillo * Swapna Behera
Tezmin Ition Tsai * Eliza Segiet * William S. Peters, Sr.

The Year of the Poet XI
April 2024

Featured Global Poets

Hassanal Abdullah * Johny Takkedasila
Rajashree Mohapatra * Shirley Smothers

Renowned Poets

~ William Butler Yeats ~

The Poetry Posse 2024

Gail Weston Shazor * Albert Carasco * Hülya N. Yılmaz
Jackie Davis Allen * Caroline Nazareno * Mutawaf Shaheed
Alicja Maria Kuberska * Teresa E. Gallion * Noreen Snyder
Michelle Joan Barulich * Shareef Abdur – Rasheed
Ashok K. Bhargava * Elizabeth Castillo * Swapna Behera
Tezmin Ition Tsai * Eliza Segiet * William S. Peters, Sr.

Now Available

www.innerchildpress.com/the-year-of-the-poet

The Year of the Poet XI
May 2024

Featured Global Poets

Binod Dawadi * Petros Kyriakou Veloudas
Rayees Ahmad Kumar * Solomon C Jatta

Renowned Poets

~ Makhanlal Chaturvedi ~

The Poetry Posse 2024

Gail Weston Shazor * Albert Carasco * Hülya N. Yılmaz
Jackie Davis Allen * Caroline Nazareno * Mutawaf Shaheed
Alicja Maria Kuberska * Teresa E. Gallion * Noreen Snyder
Michelle Joan Barulich * Shareef Abdur – Rasheed
Ashok K. Bhargava * Elizabeth Castillo * Swapna Behera
Tezmin Ition Tsai * Eliza Segiet * William S. Peters, Sr.

The Year of the Poet XI
June 2024

Featured Global Poets

C. S. P Shrivastava * Maria Evelyn Quilla Soleta
Moulay Cherif Chebihi Hassani * Swayam Prashant

Renowned Poets

~ Langston Hughs ~

The Poetry Posse 2024

Gail Weston Shazor * Albert Carasco * Hülya N. Yılmaz
Jackie Davis Allen * Caroline Nazareno * Mutawaf Shaheed
Alicja Maria Kuberska * Teresa E. Gallion * Noreen Snyder
Michelle Joan Barulich * Shareef Abdur – Rasheed
Ashok K. Bhargava * Elizabeth Castillo * Swapna Behera
Tezmin Ition Tsai * Eliza Segiet * William S. Peters, Sr.

The Year of the Poet XI
July 2024

Featured Global Poets

Barbara Gaiardoni * Bharati Nayak
Errol Bean * Michael Lee Johnson

Renowned Poets

~ Pablo Neruda ~

The Poetry Posse 2024

Gail Weston Shazor * Albert Carasco * Hülya N. Yılmaz
Jackie Davis Allen * Caroline Nazareno * Mutawaf Shaheed
Alicja Maria Kuberska * Teresa E. Gallion * Noreen Snyder
Michelle Joan Barulich * Shareef Abdur – Rasheed
Ashok K. Bhargava * Elizabeth Castillo * Swapna Behera
Tezmin Ition Tsai * Eliza Segiet * William S. Peters, Sr.

The Year of the Poet XI
August 2024

Featured Global Poets

Ibrahim Honjo * Khalice Jade
Irma Kurti * Mennadi Farah

Renowned Poets

~ Li Bai ~

The Poetry Posse 2024

Gail Weston Shazor * Albert Carasco * Hülya N. Yılmaz
Jackie Davis Allen * Caroline Nazareno * Mutawaf Shaheed
Alicja Maria Kuberska * Teresa E. Gallion * Noreen Snyder
Michelle Joan Barulich * Shareef Abdur – Rasheed
Ashok K. Bhargava * Elizabeth Castillo * Swapna Behera
Tezmin Ition Tsai * Eliza Segiet * William S. Peters, Sr.

Now Available

www.innerchildpress.com/the-year-of-the-poet

246

The Year of the Poet XI
September 2024

Featured Global Poets

Ngozi Olivia Osuoha * Teodozja Świderska
Chinh Nguyen * Awatef El Idrissi Douklilis

Renowned Poets

~ William Ernest Henley ~

The Poetry Posse 2024

Gail Weston Shazor * Albert Carasco * Hülya N. Yılmaz
Jackie Davis Allen * Caroline Nazareno * Mutawaf Shaheed
Alicja Maria Kuberska * Teresa E. Gallion * Noreen Snyder
Michelle Joan Barulich * Shareef Abdur – Rasheed
Ashok K. Bhargava * Elizabeth Castillo * Swapna Behera
Tezmin Ition Tsai * Eliza Segiet * William S. Peters, Sr.

The Year of the Poet XI
October 2024

Featured Global Poets

Deepak Kumar Dey * Shallal 'Anour
Adnan Al-Sayegh * Taghrid Bou Merhi

Renowned Poets

~ Adam Mickiewicz ~

The Poetry Posse 2024

Gail Weston Shazor * Albert Carasco * Hülya N. Yılmaz
Jackie Davis Allen * Caroline Nazareno * Mutawaf Shaheed
Alicja Maria Kuberska * Teresa E. Gallion * Noreen Snyder
Michelle Joan Barulich * Shareef Abdur – Rasheed
Ashok K. Bhargava * Elizabeth Castillo * Swapna Behera
Tezmin Ition Tsai * Eliza Segiet * William S. Peters, Sr.

The Year of the Poet XI
November 2024

Featured Global Poets

Abraham Tawiah Tei * Neha Bhandarkar
Zaneta Varnado Johns * Haseena Bnaiyan

Renowned Poets

~ Wole Soyinka ~

The Poetry Posse 2024

Gail Weston Shazor * Albert Carasco * Hülya N. Yılmaz
Jackie Davis Allen * Caroline Nazareno * Mutawaf Shaheed
Alicja Maria Kuberska * Teresa E. Gallion * Noreen Snyder
Michelle Joan Barulich * Shareef Abdur – Rasheed
Ashok K. Bhargava * Elizabeth Castillo * Swapna Behera
Tezmin Ition Tsai * Eliza Segiet * William S. Peters, Sr.

The Year of the Poet XI
December 2024

Featured Global Poets

Kapardeli Eftichia * Irena Jovanović
Sudipta Mishra * Til Kumari Sharma

Renowned Poets

~ Imru' al-Qais ~

The Poetry Posse 2024

Gail Weston Shazor * Albert Carasco * Hülya N. Yılmaz
Jackie Davis Allen * Caroline Nazareno * Mutawaf Shaheed
Alicja Maria Kuberska * Teresa E. Gallion * Noreen Snyder
Michelle Joan Barulich * Shareef Abdur – Rasheed * Swapna Behera
Ashok K. Bhargava * Elizabeth Castillo * Kimberly Burnham
Tezmin Ition Tsai * Eliza Segiet * William S. Peters, Sr.

Now Available

www.innerchildpress.com/the-year-of-the-poet

The Year of the Poet XII
January 2025

Featured Global Poets
Khalice Jade * Til Kumari Sharma
Sushant Thapa * Orbindu Ganga

 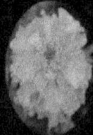 

Innocence	Joy	Longing
Daisy	Marigold	Camellia

The Poetry Posse 2025

Gail Weston Shazor * Albert Carasco * Hülya N. Yılmaz
Jackie Davis Allen * Caroline Nazareno * Mutawaf Shaheed
Alicja Maria Kuberska * Teresa E. Gallion * Noreen Snyder
Shareef Abdur – Rasheed * Swapna Behera * Eliza Segiet
Ashok K. Bhargava * Elizabeth Castillo * Kimberly Burnham
Tzemin Ition Tsai * William S. Peters, Sr.

The Year of the Poet XII
February 2025

Featured Global Poets
Shafkat Aziz Hajam * Frosina Tasevska
Muhammad Gaddafi Masoud * Karen Morrison

 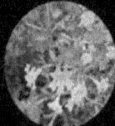 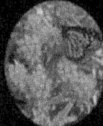

Curiosity	Fear	Lonlines
Hibiscus	Minulus	Butterfly Weed

The Poetry Posse 2025

Gail Weston Shazor * Albert Carasco * Hülya N. Yılmaz
Jackie Davis Allen * Caroline Nazareno * Mutawaf Shaheed
Alicja Maria Kuberska * Teresa E. Gallion * Noreen Snyder
Shareef Abdur – Rasheed * Swapna Behera * Eliza Segiet
Ashok K. Bhargava * Elizabeth Castillo * Kimberly Burnham
Tzemin Ition Tsai * William S. Peters, Sr.

The Year of the Poet XII
March 2025

Featured Global Poets

Deepak Kumar Dey * Binod Dawadi
Faleeha Hassan * Kapardeli Eftichia

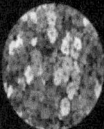 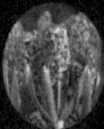 

Frustration	Sorrow	Detrmination
Petunias	Purple Hyacinth	Amaryllis

The Poetry Posse 2025

Gail Weston Shazor * Albert Carasco * Hülya N. Yılmaz
Jackie Davis Allen * Caroline Nazareno * Mutawaf Shaheed
Alicja Maria Kuberska * Teresa E. Gallion * Noreen Snyder
Shareef Abdur – Rasheed * Swapna Behera * Eliza Segiet
Ashok K. Bhargava * Elizabeth Castillo * Kimberly Burnham
Tzemin Ition Tsai * William S. Peters, Sr.

The Year of the Poet XII
April 2025

Featured Global Poets

Gopal Sinha * Taghrid Bou Merhi
Irma Kurti * Marlon Salem Gruezo

  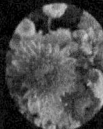

Resilience	Self Doubt	Grief
Calendula	Centaury	Chrysanthemums

The Poetry Posse 2025

Gail Weston Shazor * Albert Carasco * Hülya N. Yılmaz
Jackie Davis Allen * Caroline Nazareno * Mutawaf Shaheed
Alicja Maria Kuberska * Teresa E. Gallion * Noreen Snyder
Shareef Abdur – Rasheed * Swapna Behera * Eliza Segiet
Ashok K. Bhargava * Elizabeth Castillo * Kimberly Burnham
Tzemin Ition Tsai * William S. Peters, Sr.

Now Available

www.innerchildpress.com/the-year-of-the-poet

and there is much, much more !

visit . . .

www.innerchildpress.com/antho
logies-sales-special.php

Also check out our Authors and
all the wonderful Books
Available at :

www.innerchildpress.com/autho
rs-pages

World Healing World Peace 2022

Poets for Humanity

Now Available

www.worldhealingworldpeacepoetry.com

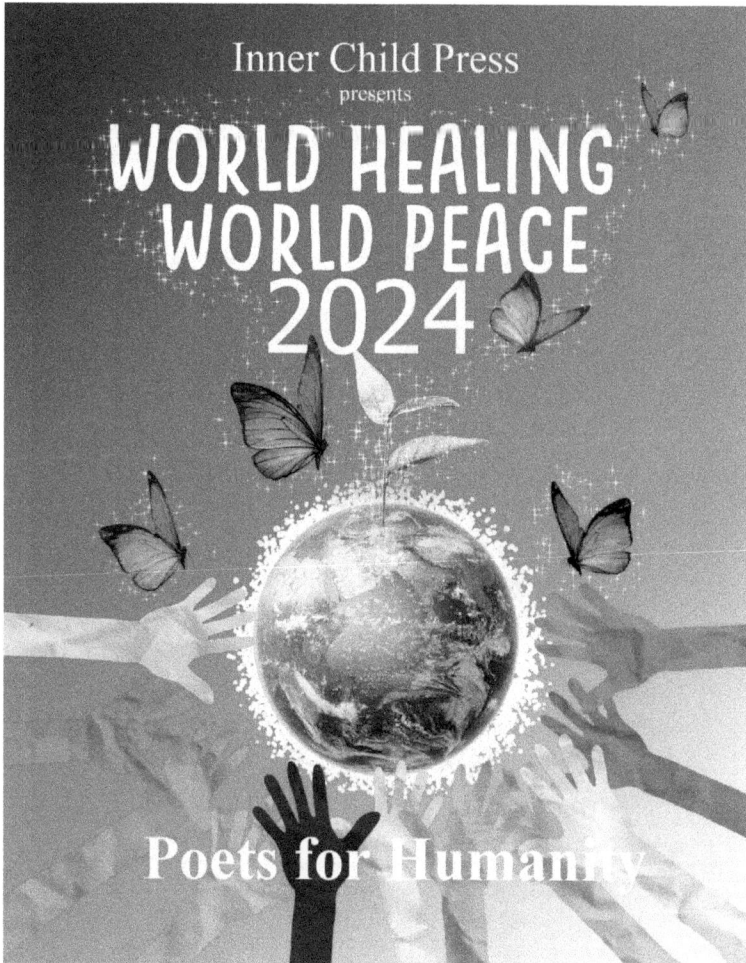

Inner Child Press
presents

WORLD HEALING
WORLD PEACE
2024

Poets for Humanity

Now Available

www.worldhealingworldpeacepoetry.com

World Healing World Peace
2020

Poets for Humanity

Now Available

www.worldhealingworldpeacepoetry.com

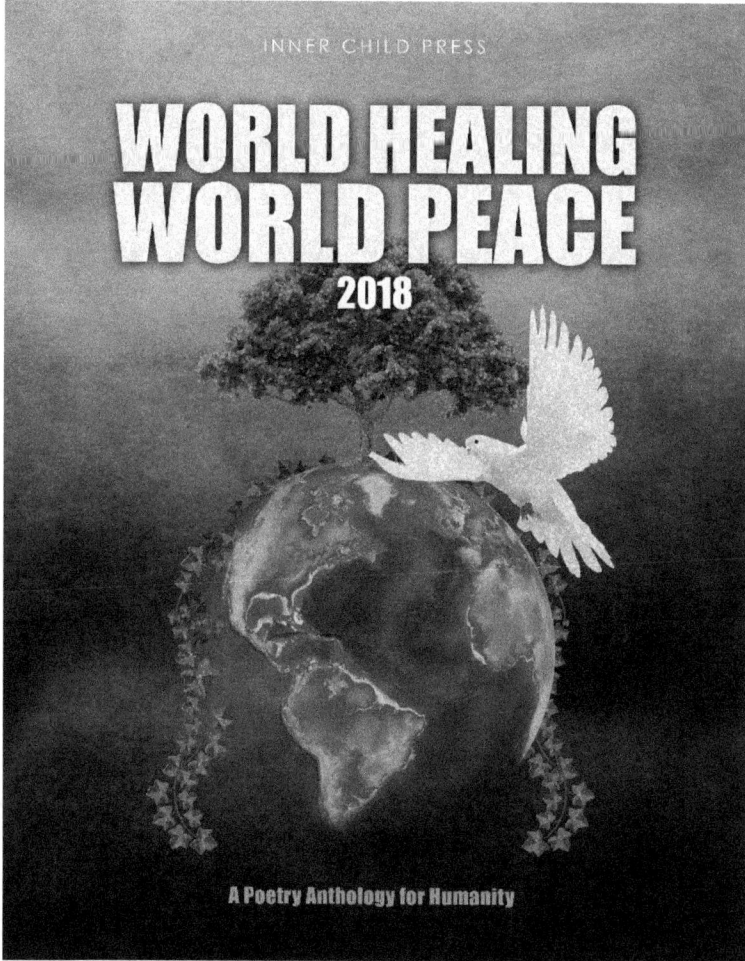

INNER CHILD PRESS

WORLD HEALING
WORLD PEACE
2018

A Poetry Anthology for Humanity

Now Available

www.worldhealingworldpeacepoetry.com

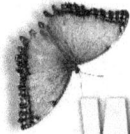

I support

World Healing
World Peace

www.worldhealingworldpeacepoetry.com

254

World Healing World Peace

Poetry

i am a believer!

World Healing
World Peace
2012, 2014, 2016, 2018,
2020, 2022, 2024

Now Available

www.worldhealingworldpeacepoetry.com

Inner Child Press International

'building bridges of cultural understanding'

Meet the Board of Directors

William S. Peters, Sr.
Chair Person
Founder
Inner Child Enterprises
Inner Child Press

Hülya N Yılmaz
Director
Editing Services
Co-Chair Person

Fahredin B. Shehu
Director
Cultural Affairs

Elizabeth E. Castillo
Director
Recording Secretary

De'Andre Hawthorne
Director
Performance Poetry

Gail Weston Shazor
Director
Anthologies

Kimberly Burnham
Director
Cultural Ambassador
Pacific Northwest
USA

Ashok K. Bhargava
Director
WIN Awards

Deborah Smart
Director
Publicity
Marketing

Khalice Jade
Director
Translation
Services

www.innerchildpress.com

256

Inner Child Press International

'building bridges of cultural understanding'

Meet our Cultural Ambassadors

Fahredin Shehu
Director of Cultural

Faleha Hassan
Iraq - USA

Elizabeth E. Castillo
Philippines

Antoinette Coleman
Chicago
Midwest USA

Ananda Nepali
Nepal - Tibet
Northern India

Kimberly Burnham
Pacific Northwest
USA

Alicja Kuberska
Poland
Eastern Europe

Swapna Behera
India
Southeast Asia

Kolade O. Freedom
Nigeria
West Africa

Munsif Beroual
Morocco
Northern Africa

Ashok K. Bhargava
Canada

Tzemin Ition Tsai
Republic of China
Greater China

Alicia M. Ramírez
Mexico
Central America

Christena AV Williams
Jamaica
Caribbean

Louise Hudon
Eastern Canada

Aziz Mountassir
Morocco
Northern Africa

Shareef Abdur-Rasheed
Southeastern USA

Laure Charazac
France
Western Europe

Mohammad Ikbal Harb
Lebanon
Middle East

Mohamed Abdel Aziz Shmeis
Egypt
Middle East

Hilary Mainga
Kenya
Eastern Africa

Josephus R. Johnson
Liberia

Mennadi Farah
Algeria

www.innerchildpress.com

257

This Anthological Publication
is underwritten solely by

Inner Child Press International

Inner Child Press is a Publishing Company
Founded and Operated by Writers. Our
personal publishing experiences provides
us an intimate understanding of the
sometimes daunting challenges Writers,
New and Seasoned may face in the
Business of Publishing and Marketing
their Creative "Written Work".

For more Information

Inner Child Press International

www.innerchildpress.com

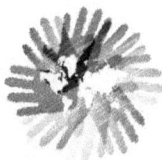

'building bridges of cultural understanding'

www.innerchildpress.com

202 Wiltree Court, State College, Pennsylvania 16801

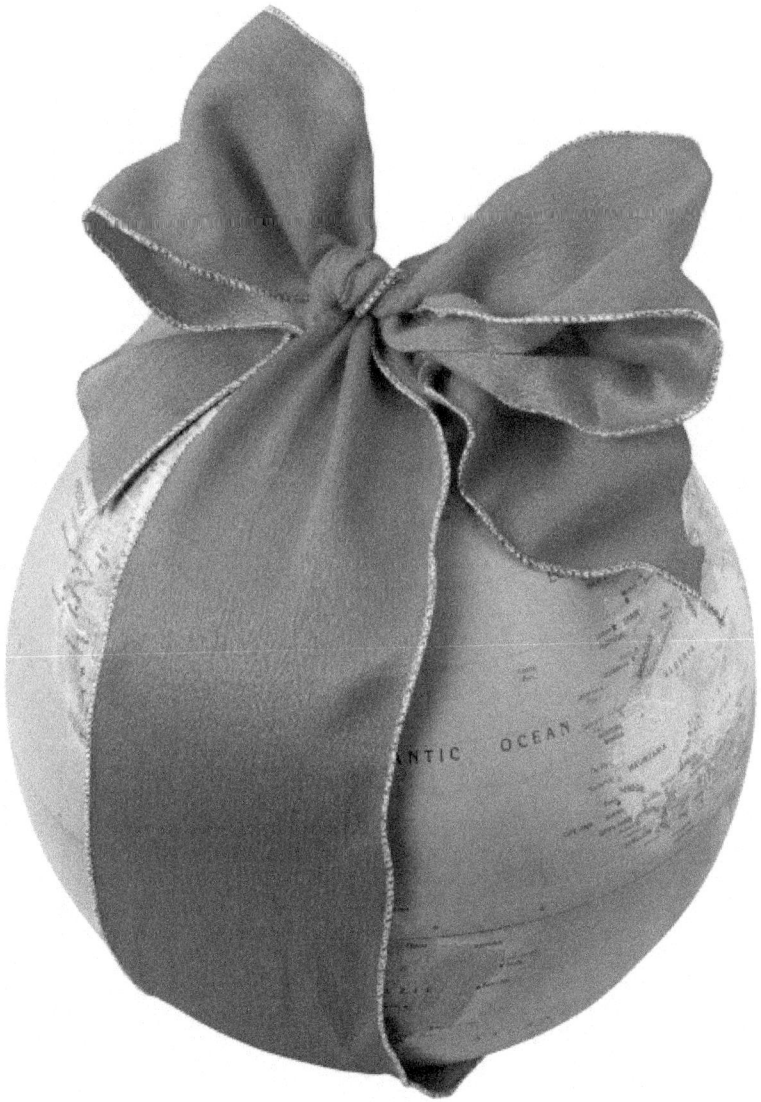

This is our world . . .

~ fini ~

www.ingramcontent.com/pod-product-compliance
Lightning Source LLC
LaVergne TN
LVHW051041080426
835508LV00019B/1634